COMPELLING
CIVIC INTEREST

INDICTMENT
OF A
GRAND JURY
"It Can Happen To You"

By
DICK FOSTER
A TRUE STORY

Affiliated Writers of America / Encampment, Wyoming

ISBN: 1-879915-12-X
Library of Congress Catalog Card Number:

DEDICATION

This book is written with the full intention of the author to place principles and ethics above personalities, and is dedicated to my wife, Dorothy, and my three children, Judy, Trudy, and Jeff.

COMPELLING CIVIC INTEREST

FOREWORD

There have been three major disasters in my life. Two of them were the loss of two grandchildren, one in a drowning, and one in a motorcycle accident.

The drowning was my grandson Eric. He was five years old, and he, along with two of my other grandchildren, was playing at Wade's Trailer Park in Laramie. My mother-in-law, Helen Olson, was babysitting them at the time. They went outside to play and they approached an old, closed-up building which had a swimming pool in it which had been abandoned. The water in the pool was loaded with chlorine, and so murky you couldn't see the bottom of the pool.

The three children had somehow gotten into this building. One of them had thrown a shoe into the pool, and apparently Eric jumped in to try to get the shoe back. The pool was so full of chlorine that the minute he hit the water he was in trouble. Just one mouthful had made it impossible for him to breathe. He could swim, but not in that water. When Helen tried to find the kids to get them back inside the house, she only found the younger two. She asked them where Eric was and one of them said, "He's in the swimming pool."

Helen had the children take her to this swimming pool, but the water was so murky that she couldn't see the bottom at the deep end. She didn't see Eric and wondered where he was. So she called my daughter Judy, Eric's mother, and called the corner where I was working, which was not very far from the trailer court. One of my employees had taken the call and came to me and said, "Mr. Foster, I hate to tell you this, but you may have just lost a grandson in a drowning in a swimming pool."

Upon hearing this, I asked the employee where she had gotten this information, and did she know more? She said, "No, I was just told you need to get to Wade's Trailer Court as quick as you possibly can."

I jumped in my car and went immediately to Wade's, which was only five minutes away. By the time I got there, Judy, who had also been contacted, showed up, too. The two of us immediately went to the pool to check to see if he was in there, but we couldn't tell. We could see the bottom everywhere but at the deep end. I didn't jump in on the spot because it had been too long to save him at this point, even if he were in there. Of course we were hoping he wasn't.

So we went back to grandma's trailer keeping in mind that he may be around the trailer park someplace. I told Judy I was going to walk around the park and see if I could find him. So I walked back toward the pool, looking around, and then I got to the pool and went into the building one more time to see if I could see him. I was still unable to see little Eric, but I knew I could not have seen him if he were in the deep end. So I looked around and found a long pole and started probing in the water at the deep end. My heart sunk as I felt the pole hit something. I knew at that point it was little Eric. And also knew it was far beyond any chance of his survival.

So I went back to the trailer, knowing that I had to tell my daughter that he was at the bottom of the pool. As I told Judy, I said, "Judy, Eric is in the pool." And I could see the despair and anguish immediately, and she dropped to the floor on her knees and started moaning, and the only thing I could do was get on the floor with her and hold her in my arms. My despair was at a very high pitch but I knew hers would have been even greater. So all I could do for a period of thirty minutes was hold her and let her weep.

The second disaster was the loss of my grandson Dustin, who was the son of Warren, and the stepson of my daughter Judy, who along with Warren, had raised Dustin from a very young age. Dustin was nearly sixteen when his dad decided to buy him a motorcycle so they could ride motorbikes together.

One day when he was coming home from school on his motorcycle, he was on Curtis Street and a semi-truck was pulling off the southbound lane of the interstate onto Curtis. Coming from the east, Dustin came up a small incline as he approached and topped the bridge over the interstate, and would have been unable to see the truck until he got to the top of the bridge, which in this case, was too late for him to stop. It was learned later that Dustin only had his rear wheel brake to try to stop with because the front wheel brake handle had been recently broken. He and the motorcycle collided near the rear axles of the belly-dump trailer. It is believed that Dustin only had seconds of hope, while he skidded in a straight line for about 190 feet, that the truck and trailer would clear the right lane in time for him to pass free of collision and behind the truck's trailer. But the window of escape closed on Dustin.

Of course the ambulance had been called, and I found out by phone that Dustin had been in an accident and had been taken to Ivinson Memorial Hospital in Laramie. The hospital determined that although Dustin had been wearing a full face helmet, it was possible that he had a severe head injury. Warren and Judy were given hope at the hospital, but because of concern for the head injury, it was recommended that Dustin be transported by "Flight for Life" to the Neuro Intensive Care Unit at Poudrc Valley Hospital in Fort Collins, Colorado. When I got to Ivinson hospital, I talked with Warren and Judy for only a short time before Dustin was to be airlifted. As Warren and Judy watched them prepare Dustin for his ride in the helicopter, all I could do was simply ask them to keep me posted as to Dustin's condition.

That night, Dustin went through surgery at Fort Collins for removal of his ruptured spleen and setting of a broken leg. Although he had a respirator, he was breathing on his own but the extent of the head injury remained unknown. The next morning tests were taken that showed no brain waves, which meant that Dustin's life was being artificially sustained with no chance for recovery. It was quite apparent that when the life support system would be removed, it would only be seconds until his life would end. It was decided that Dustin would wish to have his organs donated as a gift of life, and so it was. What I'll always remember is Judy and Warren as they walked down the hall to see Dustin for the last time. It reminded me of the same despair I'd felt when Judy had lost little Eric. And my heart went out to Warren.

The third disaster occured the evening that I lay in my motorhome in Saratoga, Wyoming, after having spent the day in front of the Laramie grand jury, and seeing my family business, Foster's Country Corner, shown on television, along with the story that I, my son Jeff, and my daughter Trudy, had been indicted by the grand jury for blackmail. I felt almost the same feeling of despair which I'd felt when I lost my two grandsons. You would think they would at least have had the decency to notify us first, rather than have us learn about it watching the evening television news. But they didn't.

I had learned to cope with the first two disasters. These had been accidents. And only God knows why these happened. And so, it was with God that I rested my soul on the matter, and prayed for the souls of my lost loved ones. This I was able to do, and really, it was what I had to do. It was all I could do. It is all anyone can do. These incidents require trust in God, and faith that it was His decision and had to be for some reason unkown to man. I learned to cope with this, and this is how.

The third disaster, however, was markedly different. It was no accident. Further, I do not believe it was divine in nature. And as the last twelve years have transpired, I have been unable to cope with this third disaster, with what I feel was caused by a set of acts by certain elected officials, and others in their control, to destroy myself and my family and our business in Laramie. To try to understand why these people made this happen perplexes me yet today.

Now the fact that the legal system allowed this to happen, the whole affair in its entirety, including the fact that all parties were immune from any responsibility afterward, has caused me further anguish. I am a believer in our American system of justice in general. But without honesty and integrity within that system, we have nothing. There is a big hole into which the whole concept of justice disappears.

I have made the decision to write this book so that I can reveal to the public just how all this came about, in the best detail I can recall and document, so that I may once and for all, "Let go, and let God."

COMPELLING CIVIC INTEREST

CHAPTER ONE

I was in Hawaii when my son-in-law, Warren, called me from Laramie, Wyoming and said, "They just picked up Rex Guice and charged him with seven counts of gasoline price fixing. Thought you should know."

This really didn't mean anything to me at the moment. But as it sank in, I wondered what he did to get charged. After all, I was in the gasoline business, too, and wanted to know what was going on in Laramie while I was away. "What did he do to get picked up?"

"They say he had approached managers of several companies with gas stations in Laramie, to get a survey of gas prices sent to their corporate offices. I guess he wanted to show that gas prices were moving up in Laramie."

I thought for a moment, and over the past two weeks there had been a gas war in Laramie and prices had dropped ten or twelve cents a gallon, which meant gas was being sold at cost, maybe even below cost. I was trying to connect this in my mind, perhaps it was related. Rex Guice operated five or six service stations in Laramie using Phillips as a supplier, and the gas war had certainly cost him money, as well as me or anybody else in the business.

The prices had gone down while I was in Hawaii, and Warren had kept me posted and had lowered prices at our stations to stay competitive. After our prices had been down and we had been selling at cost for several days, I had told Warren that I felt we had to raise our price, we had to make some kind of profit. We were at $0.98-9 and I told him to raise it to $1.09-9. I had hoped the other stations would follow suit, but now there was something else going on with Rex Guice which I just couldn't place into the picture.

I knew my competition as any business man has to to survive, and I knew Rex. His main office was right across the street from mine. Our relationship was casual and friendly, as we were business neighbors. Both of us had worked for large oil companies in the past, and we both knew how the business worked. But we had never discussed gas prices. When one of us would change price, the other would find out by looking at the sign, just like anybody else. Our price decisions were totally independent of each other. Having had this experience with Rex for eight or ten years, never having seen him do anything unethical in all that time, I couldn't imagine his doing things any differently with any of the other dealers. The only reason I could think of for him to talk with other dealers about a survey of price would be a reaction to the fact that many competitors were based out of town. This idea of a survey, if it was his idea, perhaps, had been construed as an attempt at price fixing.

"How did you find out about this?" I asked Warren.

"It was in the newspaper. Front page. He was charged with seven counts. That's all I know. That's basically all it says."

One side of me felt that since I was not involved in this, that it wouldn't affect me or my business. But another side of me thought, if they're after him, and I'm right across the street, they're not going to stop with him. If they arrested Rex, it would be likely that the whole industry in Laramie would be scrutinized. And I knew that the public felt that gas prices had been too high ever since the controversial gas shortages of 1973. I didn't think the public would ever get over this, this would always be with America. So any allegation of impropriety in this business was going to be hot news. Unfortunately, it was small independent dealers such as myself and Rex Guice who usually took the brunt of this public sentiment toward the industry. That alone was almost enough to make you feel like a criminal just because you're selling gas.

Myself, I was proud. Because I had started pumping gas for Standard Oil Company in San Jose, California, when I was twenty years old. And with a lot of hard work and determination, finally started my own station, and kept working to build more. One of the things I had always done was work honestly. I had never taken advantage of anyone, and felt that it was the worst thing you could do in life. I felt my success was due in large part to my integrity, and I raised my family on the same principles.

Well, there was no use thinking about this any more from Hawaii. So I let it go for the time being and continued my vacation with my wife, Dorothy.

We had a condominium there which we had bought in 1972 on the Kona Coast, on the Big Island. It was a beautiful place on the sixteenth green of the Kona Golf Course, and on out to the ocean where you could watch the ships go by.

All in all, though, I had a slight feeling of foreboding on my return home and hoped things wouldn't go too badly for Rex. I felt if he was in trouble, he probably didn't deserve it. We came home as planned, on or about March 20, 1983.

When I got back to Laramie it was a clear, warm day for that time of year. I went to the office in the morning and met with Warren. There hadn't been anything new in the papers as near as I could tell. So I guessed that nothing more was happening.

I went to see Rex Guice straightaway because I was concerned about him and when I saw him I said, "Rex, I don't believe you're guilty of this charge. I just wanted you to know how I feel." I did this in spite of the possibility that someone might see me go to him and think this was another conspiracy. After all, he was a marked man. Other people in the business would go out of their way to avoid him for fear of accusation, but I felt it was important for him to know how I felt, and that I respected him. He thanked me for this support, and believe me, he needed it.

Then, in a couple of days, the word was out in rumors that the district attorney wanted to call a grand jury to scrutinize the gasoline business in Laramie. The first word I got of this came from Warren. My son-in-law worked for me but was also an attorney. And later, I heard something else from Warren that absolutely shocked me. He had been to the court house and had been met by Hoke MacMillan, who is also an attorney in Laramie, and an ex-partner of our district judge, the Honorable Arthur T. Hanscum. MacMillan informed Warren, "You better tell Dick to get an attorney. He's going to need one."

"Where did you get this?" Warren had asked.

MacMillan wouldn't say, other than he had just "heard it."

So now my feeling of foreboding was coming to substance. I suspected this would blow out into an industry-wide investigation, but I really didn't believe that in all my years of doing business in Laramie that people would think I was operating illegally. The idea of being accused of a crime didn't sit well with me. Being told you are going to need an attorney makes you look back and think, what have I done? Well, as far as I could look, I hadn't done anything wrong since before I quit drinking on June 20, 1956. I had sat in jail for a DUI in San Jose, California, and decided I'd done enough drinking, and it was time for me to change my life. And I did. It was an important decision, which one day at a time, I've been able to maintain. The only possibility for MacMillan's meaning with his comment had to be related to somebody trying to implicate me in this gasoline price fixing. I was probably the biggest

6

independent gas dealer in Laramie (the biggest are the oil companies, and nobody is going to go after them), so perhaps I would become the target of an investigation, too. I was the most visible in the community, and visibly successful, and if they wanted a scapegoat, I guessed I would be the most valuable one for them to pursue. So I waited, wondering what would happen next.

COMPELLING CIVIC INTEREST

CHAPTER TWO

It was about a month from the time the district attorney decided he'd like to have a grand jury—until he had one. The proper procedures and authority require several steps. First, approval by the county commissioners must be sought because of the undue expense which may be incurred by the county. After that, a prosecutor must make formal request to the district judge, in this case, Arthur T. Hanscum, and with his final approval, a grand jury can be called.

The letter to the judge had been sent on April Fool's Day,

1983, by Richard E. Dixon, Deputy County and Prosecuting Attorney, working under the authority of Karen Maurer, County Attorney. Although I, of course, hadn't seen this at the time, I had only been able to see this after the trials were all over. Even then, the kickback report attached to the request for the grand jury was not given to me as I believe is required by law, so that I could have protected myself against the allegations. I got this only by chance, after the trials. I also later got the judge's response. The county attorney's office had a legal duty to provide me with what I call the Leazenby kickback report, which was the sole evidence used and presented to the judge to call the grand jury. But they did not do this, so I had no idea where the allegations against me were coming from.

The Leazenby kickback report is presented here so that the reader can see how this grand jury episode began in formality, and how I was implicated. Only later in this book, will the reader begin to understand the improprieties which followed from the use of this report. As is evident from the judge's response, the grand jury was called solely on the issue of public interest, and on the possible charges of price fixing. The kickback accusation was not mentioned in the judge's reply. This is important because price fixing is a misdemeanor, and kickbacks are a felony. With the information that I later received from the Wyoming Attorney General's Office, and from statements made by Judge Arthur T. Hanscum himself during the trial, misdemeanors are not sufficient reason to call a grand jury. A misdemeanor is relatively petty in criminal violations, and grand juries are very expensive to call. Thusly, a felony is required to justify the expense and procedure. The real story behind the inducement and creation of the Leazenby kickback report is one which later shocked me to the point of writing this book, as it is the fulcrum upon which the grand jury was called and upon which the ultimate verdict would be cast.

April 1, 1983

Karen Maurer, County & Prosecuting Attorney
Richard E. Dixon, Deputy
Tony S. Lopez, Deputy
Office of Albany County and Prosecuting Attorney
525 Grand Avenue - Suite 304
Albany County Courthouse
Laramie, Wyoming 82070
(307) 745-4849

The Honorable Arthur T. Hanscum
525 Grand Avenue
Courthouse, Suite 303
Laramie, Wyoming 82070

Dear Judge Hanscum:

COMPELLING CIVIC INTEREST

On March 15, 1983, a complaint and warrant were issued for Lyndol Rex Guice charging seven counts of "attempted unfair discrimination" in violation of Wyoming Statutes S40-4-202(1977). It is alleged that Mr. Guice, a local Phillips 66 "jobber", went about Laramie attempting to coerce retailers for several different brands of gasoline into agreeing to raise their prices for self-serve regular gas from 98.9 cents a gallon to 109.9 cents a gallon. In at least one instance, Mr. Guice is charged with telephoning a District Manager for Pester Gasoline in Denver, Colorado, in order to enlist "cooperation" at that level with the plan to move gas prices in Laramie 11% higher. It is the view of Albany County Sheriff, Don Fritzen, who is in charge of the ongoing investigation, that Mr. Guice was acting as an agent for a local cartel of gasoline wholesaler / retailers who have been involved for some time in an ongoing conspiracy to control the price of gas in Laramie, contrary to law. These men wield considerable economic power over employees and their dependents as well as the gas-buying public. Cooperation with the authorities, outside the context of grand jury proceedings, could mean the loss of economic livelihood for many potential witnesses.

The formidable power and arrogance of the targets of our ongoing investigation combined with the pandemic impact of artificially elevated gasoline prices make this matter one which, in my view, is eminently well suited to the prosecutorial instrumentality of a grand jury. Informal discussions with the Albany County Commissioners have yielded a favorable response to a proposed country-wide[sic] grand jury. The purpose of this letter is to briefly outline the history and workings or[sic] a grand jury and, at your request, to discuss the limitations and drawbacks of covening such a body.

Grand juries originated with the English King Henry II's Assize of

Clarendon in 1166.[1] They were, originally, revenue sharing devices and counters to the dominance of ecclesiastical courts.[2] In time, they evolved into a citizens' safeguard against the excesses of royal power and come to stand between prosecutor and accused to ensure that the prosecutor did not bring charges based on ill-will or unbelievable testimony. Hale v. Henkel, 201 U.S. 43 at 59, 50 L.Ed. 652 at 659, 26 S.Ct 370 (1905)

The primary role of the present day grand jury is to assess the State's evidence against a suspect to determine if probable cause exists sufficient to merit a trial on the merits. Bracy v. United States, 435 U.S. 1301 at 1302, 55 L.Ed. 2nd 489 at 491, 98 S.Ct. 1171(1978). Use of a grand jury for "fishing expeditions" can prove disastrous as was recently demonstrated in Wyoming when a state-wide grand jury was covened at a cost of some three quarters of a million dollars with negligible results. But, as in the instant case, when a solid foundation has been laid with competent investigation, the grand jury can prove invaluable as a source of sworn testimony from key witnesses who might otherwise be effectively restrained from offering their assistance to the investigation. The value of the long established tradition of secrecy in grand jury proceedings has been well summarized by our nation's Supreme Court:

> First, if preindictment proceedings were made public, many prospective witnesses would be hesitant to come forward voluntarily, knowing that those against whom they testify would

---

[1]W. Holdsworth, HISTORY OF ENGLISH LAW, 321 (7th Rev. Ed. 1956)

[2]T. Plucknett, A CONCISE HISTORY OF THE COMMON LAW, 110 (4th Ed. 1948)

be aware of that testimony; second, witnesses who appeared before the grand jury would be less likely to testify fully and frankly, as they would be open to retribution as well as to inducements; third, there also would be the risk that those about to be indicted would flee, or would try to influence grand jurors to vote against indictment; and finally, by preserving the secrecy of the proceedings, we assure that persons who are accused but exonerated by the grand jury will not be held up to public ridicule. Douglas Oil Co. v. Petrol Stops Northwest, 441 U.S. 211 at 219, 60 L.Ed. 2nd 156 at 165, 99 S.Ct. 1667 (1979)

The Douglas Oil case was, interestingly enough, concerned with a conspiracy to fix gasoline prices. That the quoted language has a direct application to the instant case is amply demonstrated by a review of the Sheriff's Office Supplemental Report appended hereto as Exhibit "A".

You, as District Court Judge, have sole authority to call an Albany County Grand Jury under Wyoming Statutes S7-5-101 (1977). But the grand jury originated before the Constitution and because of that pre-constitutional status it is, theoretically, independent of any governmental branch, including the judiciary which creates it. United States v. Calandra, 414 U.S. 338 at 342-343, 38L.Ed. 2nd 561 at 568, 94 S.ct 613 (1974). In fact, "tradition and the dynamics of the constitutional scheme of separation of powers define a limited function for both court and prosecutor in their dealings with the grand jury." United States v. Chanen, 549 F.2d 1306 at 1312 (9th Cir. 1977). It is this independence, coupled with an uncannily accurate reflection of community values and ideals, which I see as, perhaps, the strongest selling point for the concept of a county-wide grand jury. In Platte County, I strove to impress upon the grand jury that they were not impanelled to do Judge Taylor's bidding, nor my own;

rather I urged them to bring their own sense of justice to bear upon the information presented.

Certainly, at least at the outset, a grand jury is effectively at the mercy of the prosecutor who has subpoenaed the initial group of witnesses and conducts the initial direct examinations of those witnesses. However, at the close of each direct examination by the prosecutor, the grand jurors take over and, in my experience, generally ask more and frequently better questions of the witnesses. Moreover, the grand jury should be free to request the appearance of additional subsequent witnesses whose identities or value have come to light in the course of the initial presentation.

Giving the grand jury its own head is an essential safeguard against the general fear that a grand jury is little more than the unwitting tool of an ambitious prosecutor who, otherwise, lacks a solid case. My experiences in Platte County as well as my feel for the public mood strongly suggest that it would be difficult, if not impossible, to select a grand jury today in Albany County which would be at all disposed to cater to the whims of some Machiavellian prosecutor. Furthermore, as a practical matter, it should be emphasized that a prosecutor will seldom, if ever, advise a grand jury to return an indictment unless there is confidence that the case appears strong enough to convince a twelve man criminal jury of the suspect's quilt[sic], beyond a reasonable doubt. To the extend[sic] that the prosecutor does occupy the catbird's seat in grand jury proceedings, there is little time or opportunity to become intoxicated with real or perceived power. If the investigation hits a dead end, as did the state-wide affair some five years ago, then the prosecutor will likely become the object of no small amount of public ridicule. If, on the contrary, substantial indictments are returned, then the prosecutor's office must shoulder responsibility for successful resolution of the cases involved. When the public, in the form of a grand jury, brings indictments there is a unique and unusually intense pressure upon the prosecutor to prevail at the subsequent trials.

"The investigation of crime by the grand jury implements a fundamental governmental role of securing the safety of the person and property of the citizen." Branzburg v. Hayes, 408 U.S. 665 at 700, 33L.Ed. 2nd 626 at 650, 92 S.Ct. 2646 (1972). Why, in the instant case, is a grand jury better suited to press forward with the investigation than the more traditionally charged Sheriff's and County Attorney's Offices? First, it should be noted that there has been no abdication of responsibility by either of those offices in this case. Rather, the grand jury would be in the position of "standing on the shoulders" of the Sheriff's investigation with the assistance and advice of the County Attorney.

It is the virtual universality of the demand for gasoline that makes the grand jury so uniquely qualified in this case. The need to "fill 'er up" impinges upon our daily existences more regularly than does any other need save that for food. Only the truly destitute in our society do not travel regularly by automobile. Check with Wyatt Skaggs and you will find that many, if not most, of his clients, whose legal services are being provided by the state, still manage to find the wherewithall to get around by car. So this is a "people's" issue in that it cuts across virtually every strata of society. Wide variations in the price of an essential commodity such as gasoline make a very real difference in the lives of most everyone living in Laramie.

The issue is, likewise, very real to local merchants who must compete with the lure of shopping malls and volume buying in Fort Collins and Cheyenne. I have been told by several people since this investigation started, that they can pay for a trip to Cheyenne or Fort

Collins by the savings in filling their gas tank at prices fifteen to twenty cents below the Laramie market! Thus, the price discrimination we suffer as gasoline purchasers in Laramie serves to encourage the flight of dollars earned in Laramie to the enrichment of distant markets and the relative depression of the local economy.

Clearly, my zeal in advocating a grand jury for Albany County is grounded in an appreciation for the investigatory powers possessed by such a body. That these powers are necessary in this case is, I think, adequately demonstrated by Exhibit "A" and reinforced by the formidable retaliatory measures and means of accomplishing those measures available to the prospective targets of our investigation. The grand jury, traditionally, has been recognized by our Courts as an important instrument of effective law enforcement by virtue of its investigatory powers. Branzburg v. Hayes, 408 U.S. 665 at 701, 33 L.Ed 2nd 626 at 650, 92 S.Ct. 2646 (1972).

In this case, there is an especially strong need for a thorough and comprehensive investigation. Certainly, it has been recognized that "When the grand jury is performing its investigatory function into a general problem area . . . society's interest is best served by a thorough and extensive investigation." Wood v. Georgia, 370 U.S. 375 at 392, 8 L.Ed. 2nd 569 at 581-582, 82 S.Ct. 1364 (1962). As of this writing, Mr. Lyndol Rex Guice stands in the position of a sacrificial lamb. This is not only my perception but a concern which Mr. Guice's attorney, John Scott, has already shared with me, and upon inquiry, would share with the Court. The comprehensive kind of probe which could only be effected through a grand jury might serve to properly apportion responsibility if, indeed, there is some sort of illegal price structure being forced upon the Laramie market. A grand jury investigation "is not fully carried out until every available clue has been run down and all witnesses examined in every

17

proper way to find if a crime has been committed." <u>United States v. Stone</u>, 429 F.2d 138 at 140 (2d Cir. 1970). Such an investigation may be triggered by tips, rumors, evidence proffered by the prosecutor, or the personal knowledge of the grand jurors. <u>Costello v. United States</u>, 350 U.S. 359 at 362, 100 L.Ed. 397 at 402, 76 S.Ct. 406 (1956).

In summary, the County Attorney's office proposes that a grand jury be called to look into the issues and allegations arising out of gasoline price-fixing charges which have already been formally lodged against one local individual. Such a probe would be predicted upon extensive investigative information already developed by the Albany County Sheriff's office which tends to implicate many more parties than the one thus far charged. The power and arrogance of these potential targets make the grand jury uniquely well-suited to carrying forward the delicate and difficult task of a continuing investigation. Because gas prices affect almost everyone and because they play such a pivotal role in the health of the local economy, a citizen's panel would have a dual impetus for pressing forward. The implicit perils in misuse or poor use of such a tool serve as safeguards against ill-advised use of a grand jury by the County Attorney who would act as its legal advisor.

Not surprisingly, many of the strongest arguments in favor of a grand jury can also be employed by those who would oppose calling such a body. The primary concern of opponents is that the large and secret powers of grand juries have often proved to be terrifying weapons in the hands of self-righteous or cynical prosecutors. This concern is hightened[sic] by the fact that witnesses submit themselves to grand jury testimony without the protection of an attorney, albeit still cloaked with their Fifth Amendment privilage[sic] against self-incrimination. I would counter these complaints by pointing out that a grand jury is not an adversary hearing in which the ultimate guilt or innocence of the accused is adjudicated. Rather, it is an ex parte investigation to determine whether a crime has been committed and whether criminal proceedings should be instituted against any person. United States v. Calandra, 414 U.S. 338 at 343-344, 38 L.Ed. 2d 561 at 569, 94 S.Ct. 613 (1975).

Opponents of the grand jury system argue that there have been too many cases in which witnesses have been badgered, trapped, subjected to harsh, sudden, and wearing appearances in distant places, or otherwise scarred by gratuitously high handed or perverse employment of the grand jury's great authority.[3] In the first instance, I would argue that the Albany County Attorney's office, as presently constituted, is neither equiped[sic] nor disposed to manipulate a county-wide grand jury into such a tool of oppression. In fact, I would argue that, left to regulate themselves, most prosecutors would exercise their powers responsibly.

However, excesses which came to light regarding Federal Grand Jury practices during the Nixon years[4] as well as common sense would strongly suggest that the protection of individual rights cannot solely depend upon the good faith of the prosecutor. Perhaps the answer lies in balancing the need for a grand jury in any given situation against the potential for abuse of its considerable powers. In that light, I would argue that the preceeding pages of this letter make a good case for a "compelling civic interest" in the calling of a grand jury in

---

[3]M. Frankel & G. Naftalis, THE GRAND JURY: AN INSTITUTION ON TRIAL, 117 (1977)

[4]See generally "Federal Grand Jury Investigation of Political Dissidents" 7 HARV. CIV. RIGHTS - CIV. LIB. REV. 432 (1972)

Albany County which makes the possible risks involved acceptable. Moreover, in the instant case, those powerful individuals who might well be targets of a grand jury inquiry would seem to be exercising excessive and unfettered power over many innocent individuals for the purpose of obfuscation and in an unscrupulous attempt to whitewash what would seem to be major violations of state law.

In my attempt to present the broad outlines of the cases for and against a county-wide grand jury, I have, necessarily, avoided some procedural questions which would need to be resolved before a grand jury could be called. These include whether or not to record the proceedings, availability of any such records, the possibility of grants of immunity, and like questions. I am certainly available to discuss these important considerations with you at any time.

Thank you for your time and attention to this matter.

Sincerely,

Richard E. Dixon
Deputy County and Prosecuting
Attorney

RED/ml

[EXHIBIT A follows, which was attached to the above letter]

[EXHIBIT A]

ALBANY COUNTY SHERIFF'S DEPARTMENT

SUPPLEMENTAL REPORT: C#__83-0583___PAGE:_one_____

DATE OF REPORT:__3-22-83_____OFFICER:Leazenby 520

On 3-21-83 at approximately 1215 hours I contacted Kevin Dooley, the owner of the Outrider truck stop in Laramie. This contact was made in the loby[sic] of the truck stop. At this time Dooley and myself had a conversation about the price fixing investigation that is being conducted by the Albany County Sheriff's Office.

At this time Dooley was not advised of his rights, as no questions were asked of him concerning this investigation. Dooley advised me that he knew that there was an investigation taking place, and also advised that he was aware that price fixing took place in Laramie. Dooley advised me that he was not envolved[sic] because he sold very little gas, most of his business was selling diesel fuel.

Dooley stated that he knew about the price-fixing and also had information as to who was envolved[sic]. However he would not divulge this information to me. He did state that if he was ever placed under oath or summoned as a witness that he would tell the truth, but at this time he did not want to tell me about it.

He did state that Rex Guice was not the one that we wanted, that there were other people that were more or less forcing him into this. He stated that he had information that Dick Foster was forcing Guice into paying him (Foster) a one cent kick-back on every gallon of gas that was sold at Guice's stations. Dooley would not elaborate on this

21

except to state that he (Dooley) had also been approached in the distant past about paying a one cent a gallon "fee" for every gallon that he sold so that he (Dooley) would not be under sold. He would not tell me who approached him on this, but I had the impression that it was Dick Foster.

Dooley stated that the way he arrived at his gas prices was to watch the rest of the stations and stay with them on the prices.

At the end of this conversation I advised Dooley that there was a possibility that a Grand Jury might be called to investigate this, or that there was a possibility that the Feds might be interested in it. I advised him that if this took place it was strong possibility that every station owner in Laramie would be called to give evidence in the matter. Dooley advised that he was aware of this, and if it happened he would have no other choice but to tell the truth.

At this point the conversation was ended.

Leazenby   520

[THE FOLLOWING LETTER OF APRIL 7, 1983 IS THE JUDGE'S RESPONSE TO RICHARD DIXON'S REQUEST FOR A GRAND JURY]

April 7, 1983

Arthur T. Hanscum, District Judge
Geri Harper, Court Reporter
The State of Wyoming
Second Judicial District
Albany County Court House
Room 303, P.O. Box 1106
Laramie, Wyoming 82070
(307) 745-3337

Mr. Richard E. Dixon
Deputy County and Prosecuting Attorney
Suite 304, Albany County Courthouse
Laramie, WY 82070
                    Re: Grand Jury

Dear Mr. Dixon:

I have reviewed your recent request that a grand jury be convened for purposes of the investigation of recent allegations that retailers or wholesalers of gasoline in the Laramie area may be manipulating the price of gasoline in violation of Wyoming State law.

I concur that there is a compelling civic interest in the issues concerning these allegations. I further concur that a grand jury would be the proper mechanism to investigate these allegations.

I have reviewed the statutory law in Wyoming, researched some of the case law, and discussed the propriety and purpose of a grand jury with other District Judges. I find from my discussions that the grand jury affords an opportunity for twelve members of the community to determine whether or not there is probable cause for a violation, such that the case should be bound over for trial. Moreover, it affords the opportunity for the citizen, against whom the allegations may be directed, to vindicate himself so as to remove any stigma associated with the suspicions which may be involved in the investigation. Therefore, I see the grand jury as having a dual purpose and to be appropriate in this specific case.

I would, however, propose to limit the inquiry of the grand jury to the matters arising out of the subject matter of this specific investigation. It is my impression from the tone of your request, that you concur.

Accordingly, will you please prepare an Order convening the grand jury in accordance with W.S. 7-5-101. Furthermore, will you please prepare an Order under W.S. 7-5-102 directing the Clerk to draw and summon a grand jury to attend before the Court. The Order should specify the number of twelve grand jurors to be drawn and the names must be drawn from jury box number 1 by the Clerk of Court.

Finally, I will be receptive to your view as to the date on which the grand jury term shall commence and the date on which you expect the investigation to conclude and the grand jury be dismissed. I am also available to discuss procedural questions which will need to be resolved prior to the convening of the session.

I should close by indicating to the County Attorney's office my concern that the grand jury sessions be conducted in an atmosphere which promotes the overriding goal of the criminal justice system -

that is to ascertain the truth. It is in this spirit of respect for the rights of the individual and the function of the County Attorney as the representative of the people of the State of Wyoming that I would request the grand jury to be conducted.

Very truly yours,

Arthur T. Hanscum
District Judge

ATH/mc

[It appears that the Leazenby Report was attached to this letter. At the bottom of page one the words "Exhibit C" appear, along with some handwriting which reads, "To supplemental brief - to be filed as soon as case assigned."]

These letters explain much about how the process got initiated, and about grand juries in general. The judge's response, which I also didn't get to see until much later, started the snowball rolling, and it came right at me. I was not allowed to know the identity of my accusers, or to even be able to confront them. It was all a secret process, and it was front-page news when the grand jury had been appointed.

With the grand jury appointment came a long wait, but gradually, subpoenas were served on basically everyone in the gasoline business in Laramie. The only exception I knew of was Dick Knight, the Mobil Oil Jobber at the time. He had six service stations in Laramie. He owned them. He was just like me. I don't think they ever called him in, maybe they did and I didn't know, but it seemed like they called everybody else in.

All the news on this whole matter was controlled 100% by the county attorney's office. When someone was called in, it was up to them as to what got printed in the newspaper. There was always news, front page, and it went on and on. You can imagine how I looked forward to getting my newspaper every morning. And of course, there was nothing I could do or say to respond to this. It was a regular condemnation to the public of the gasoline industry in its entirety, which naturally included me. So I just had to take it one day at a time, and see the next morning what new and terrible discovery had been announced by Richard Dixon, the deputy prosecuting attorney. The newspaper, of course, printed whatever information Dixon chose to give to them.

As my family members and key employees began to get subpoenas from Dixon's office to appear in front of the grand jury, I knew of course that at some point I would be called as well. But as I watched my family go, I took a good hard look at the city of Laramie, the city I had lived in and worked in and supported all my life.

I thought I knew this city, and its people, and its innermost workings. I thought about all the places and ways I had given things and my time to the community, whose newspaper condemned me, whose deputy county attorney suddenly seemed bent on proving me to be a criminal. And dragging my family into it, too. I thought, where in the world is this coming from?

I remembered making the decision to concentrate my business endeavors in Laramie, and sold off all the locations that were outside of the city of Laramie. This was quite a commitment to make. It had gotten quite difficult to be on the road all the time. To keep help and keep control of the stations was getting hard to do. So I started letting the stations go, one by one. When the leases came up I just wouldn't renew them, and the stations we had that we owned, that we had built, we sold off. Eventually, I had moved all my business to Laramie.

In the meantime the block behind Foster's Country Corner became open for sale and I made arrangements with the bank to buy that and that was added to the amount of ground that we owned on that interchange in Laramie. There was a designated street between the two blocks, the one I owned previously, and the one I bought. The street had never been opened but sewer and water went down this particular street, and someday it was the city's intent to actually open it up so traffic could go down it. But there wasn't much out there and there was really no need for the street. So I tried to make a deal with the city to purchase that, because then I wouldn't have a street between the two blocks that I had, and even though a building couldn't be built on it, it could be used for parking. I was told, however, by the city, that they didn't want to sell it; they felt they better keep it just in case they ever needed it. So I gave up for the time being.

I also had the opportunity to buy some property over on Curtis Street and made the decision to do that, putting more of my money from the sale of other locations around the state into Laramie for future development. I had made two different purchases over on Curtis Street and each one of those incurred buying some river frontage that the Laramie River went by. As

I acquired these parcels, I also acquired about a half or three quarters of a mile of river front property.

The first section of river which I acquired, I donated to the city, because they had a long term plan for green belt along the Laramie River—from what they had there then at the Territorial Prison—clear to Curtis Street. And they would like someday to have a green belt there where there can be traffic and foot traffic, and horse riding and parks along the river. So I donated the first piece that I had to them for their greenbelt project to make it possible that maybe someday they could get that job done.

The second piece I bought on Curtis Street had some more river frontage and I got to thinking, rather than to donate it, which was quite an expense, perhaps the city would be interested in trading that street I needed for this particular portion of river frontage. So I went to City Hall and made that offer and it was taken up with management and council or whatever they needed to do and they came back with a decision that they would do that, that they felt that they really wouldn't need that street after all but they'd have to keep easements there, of course. And I agreed with that, so I gave them some more greenbelt river frontage for their greenbelt and they gave me the deed to the street between the two pieces of property I had, so now I had that for a parking lot.

When I donated the river frontage to the city, I got my picture in the paper with the mayor, the city was grateful, and I was happy to have helped with the greenbelt and looked forward to its future improvement by the city.

The Wyoming Highway Department had also bought more property than they needed along the freeway near Foster's Country Corner, so when the freeway was all completed, they had about fifteen acres that bordered our corner which came up for sale and they were going to bid it out at an auction, so I went to the auction and wound up buying that parcel of ground, which was zoned for either a gravel pit or a cemetary, and which wasn't good for much of anything. But we worked with the city and got it rezoned to a property we could use. The lower part we got zoned to R2M which meant we could put in lots where you could bring in a trailer and put it on a permanent foundation to make a home out of it, so we put thirty lots in there, and the other five acres of it fit right up next to our corner. We got that zoned into B1 and B2 and it became a real good piece of property for us to lease out to other people to put their signs on, and to put our gasoline price signs on.

Now, it appeared to be the design of somebody in Laramie that those prices should be my undoing. As I thought further, past all the real estate transactions and donations, I thought to the community in general, the people, the organizations, many of whom through the years had come to me for help, and I had helped. My family and I were always very supportive of the community, and we donated quite heavily to most of the organizations that were in town. Now, I realized, all of this had made me very visible to everyone. I was the first person they thought of to help them with a project, and the first person they thought of when they thought of gasoline sales in town. So I suppose when the public read about Rex and the grand jury, in the back of their minds they must have thought about me and wondered. I could only hope that my actions in the past would speak louder than Dixon's accusations, which seemed to include me. On the positive side, there was 4-H, and United Way, and many, many others. Almost invariably, any time somebody had a project that they wanted to raise some money on, they would come to Dorothy and I and ask us if we would be willing to donate our condominium in Hawaii and let it be auctioned off and the funds could then go to the organization that auctioned it. When we did that once, it seemed like every time we turned around there was another organization that was wanting to let us give them the condo to auction and make some money as a fundraiser. My wife and I did this several times over a ten or twelve year period and every time that it was auctioned off it very seldom made under $2,000 and as high as $3,500, and this money went back into the community to the organization. We in turn of course had to keep up the expenses on the condo, property tax, and the payment we had on it, plus lights, gas and water, and sometimes repair the place which we wouldn't have had to do if we hadn't let it go out. This did bring in quite a bit of money that organizations could use for whatever it was they were doing. We let it be used an average of at least twice a year for at least twelve years, which is 24 times at an average of $2,000. This totals around $48,000, donations for organizations such as United Way and the Laramie Chamber of Commerce, the Hospital Foundation and different groups like that. Dot and I always felt that this had been a good way for us to show our support back to the community.

For many, many years my brother and I also supported 4-H quite heavily. Especially before coming into the service station business. Ercell was a rancher. I think he was a rancher still, even when he was in the service station business. That's where his heart always was. He liked cattle, he liked horses, and he was really a rancher more than a service station operator. And myself, also coming from the country, I had tendencies that way but not nearly the same as Ercell, although again because of my position in the community, I felt that it was proper that I support

4-H. So there were several times over the years that I bought animals. I had even bought the Grand Champion a couple of times. Ercell had always seemed to go after the Grand Champion lamb.

I spent four years on the city council from 1975 to 1978, and also, in 1977, I served as president of the Wyoming Oil Jobbers Association.

I can remember when they had a cancer drive out at Woods Landing. There was a gentleman out there that made what they called the Wooly Booger. This is a big, big fly, really. It's made out of wrought iron and horse hair and whatever else a guy could find in order to make a big fly. And they called it the Wooly Booger. It was the main item that they always had for auctions to try to raise money for the Big Valley, and there again we're talking about the Woods Landing area because it really was at Woods Landing at the dance hall that they held this particular fundraiser. And the very first one they had, my wife and I went out and I wanted to buy the Wooly Booger, and the money then, of course, was donated to the cancer fund. Then in later years two of my other brothers, Ercell and Bob, who are both older than I am, also bought a Wooly Booger, so among the three of us we had bought three of them over the years, and of course these were all held at Woods Landing, the place where I was raised, twenty seven miles west of Laramie, not a town really, just a cross-roads.

I was also quite involved with Cathedral Home, always doing what I could do to help out. Those are kids who had major problems in their younger lives one way or the other, and the Cathedral Home is the place for them to try to get their lives back together. There were times when I'd buy the 4-H cattle or even the Grand Champion. Rather than take it home for us to eat, I'd just pass it on and donate that steer to the Cathedral Home. And that way they had it out there and it was that much less that they had to buy for meat, and darned good meat it was, the best, and I was always glad to be able to do that.

Another one of the places that we donated to and supported, and which we also got a lot of support back from, is the University of Wyoming. I've always felt that the University being in Laramie has really been a big asset to Laramie, and we should be able to work together with them. We were members of the Cowboy Joe Club. We enjoyed the football games, the basketball games, and many of the other activities.

Then there was the Wyoming Territorial Prison. This was an old federal penitentiary that had just been sitting and going to pot for the last fifty years, and now it's become a piece of Laramie's history. Several million dollars have been spent there in the last few years to upgrade, rebuild this prison and many other ventures at the park that should be interesting to people and become a tourist stop. And when they first started this program, I felt it was a good program, and I donated heavily to help get the Territorial Prison started and off the ground.

Another one of the organizations that I belonged to was the Civil Air Patrol. I donated the use of my plane and my time to fly it when there was a search and rescue in progress. My brother, Bob, was also real active in that, even more so than myself, because of his flying years in the Navy. This was an opportunity for him to still fly without owning an airplane. So he stayed active enough in it that he was at one time even Wing Commander and was somewhat successful getting the airplanes from the government. He had helped get either four or five T-34s that the government donated to the Civil Air Patrol, and we were able to bring them into our department and use them in our search and rescue. And I might add that T-34s are completely aerobatical airplanes and even though I had no experience at it, it was a split-type airplane and a two-seater, front and back, not side-by-side. I really enjoyed flying that airplane. It was a real pleasure just to fly them, let alone looking for somebody while they're down.

As I thought back, I realized just how many programs and

aspects of Laramie life I had participated in. We felt good about helping Laramie, and felt that Laramie felt good about us. We were well-known, and as far as I knew, well-respected. But now, all of a sudden, I wondered if somehow this might be working against me. Maybe I had become too well-known. Maybe people thought I had designs about Laramie, maybe some thought I was only out for my own good. How, I can't conceive of, but if trouble was on the way with the grand jury, I guess I'd just have to watch and see. I had worked at living in such a manner that I would earn respect in the community. Whether people respected me was more important than whether they liked me. I knew from growing up in a rural area of Wyoming that not everyone is going to like you no matter what you do. And of course, there is always jealousy. But all in all, I loved the community, had all my business enterprises located there, and tried to keep the faith that my reputation would win out in the long run.

I bring these things out which I've done in the community only to show how visible I had let myself become. As you will see later in the book, I believe this helped make me a target for the grand jury. Because I believe they interpreted my community involvement as building too much influence.

CHAPTER THREE

When the sheriff delivered my subpoena ordering me to appear before the grand jury, I had four or five days notice to appear.

It was springtime in Laramie and the weather was good. The appearance was in the county courthouse near downtown on Grand Avenue. As I approached the building the gravity of the appearance began to set in, and as I think anyone in this position would have felt, I was wondering what this particular and peculiar day was going to bring.

As I went into the courtroom, the first order of business was instruction by the prosecuting attorney, Richard Dixon, in the presence of the twelve grand jurors, that the procedure of this meeting was strictly confidential, that the grand jurors were under oath to keep anything that happened there, in secret. But in his next sentence, he instructed me that I wasn't under that oath, that if I wanted to talk about what happened with the grand jury, I was free to do so. It was only the jurors who were bound to secrecy. The jurors were bound forever, as far as I know, they can never talk about this.

I took an oath to tell the truth, the oath we all know from any court proceeding. And I said the truth. I believe in the truth, in its strength, and its meaning in life. And because of my experience I had when I quit drinking, it was compulsary for me to be truthful with myself and others, because this honesty was essential for me to keep my promise to not drink.

So I had no delusions about myself as I sat there. I knew who I was and how I got where I was in life, and had nothing to hide or be ashamed of. But it was a fearful thing to be in front of such a powerful group. And I had to fight fear. With the strength I was able to acquire through the principles which I had chosen to live by, I was able to get through the fear factor.

But then, ironically, it wasn't price fixing or kickbacks that the grand jury and prosecuting attorney asked me about. It was about the gasoline business in general, like how much did it cost to dispense a gallon of gas, how much did I pay at the refinery, how much in taxes, how much in trucking? I answered all this, and in the five hours that I was there, told them everything they needed to know about how to open a gas station and run it. A three year old could have understood that the gasoline sold at that time was being sold at a very low profit, and maybe even under cost at certain times, which is also a misdemeanor by law. But this possible violation was not a concern to anyone in the legal business, because who would want to prosecute a gas dealer for selling too cheap?

This last was really brought to light by one of the grand jurors when he said, "Mr. Foster, why didn't you leave your gas prices down, so we the people, could enjoy those prices, and if you needed to make more money, raise the price of hamburgers in your restaurant?" It came to me that these people were not only looking to stick me with price fixing of gas, they were willing to fix the price of hamburgers with me to get me to lower gas prices. In the black humor of the moment, I felt like calling him a hamburger fixer in the proceedings, but no such humor would have been appreciated, I'm sure. But once again, I could see in the eleven other jurors that he was speaking for all of them, that they seemed willing to ask for anything and do anything to get gas cheaper for Laramie. The county attorney, Richard Dixon, had already instructed them that "gas prices have been too high in Laramie for years, and it was time to do something about it." They seemed desperate, the whole group, grasping at straws, and seeming to get nowhere on the criminal side of the subject, or for that matter, on any side of the subject, except that they got a darned good lesson on business.

After I had been on the stand for five hours I became frustrated. What in the world was going on here? I wasn't being asked anything about price fixing. So I wondered what they were looking for in me, and said to the jury, "Hey. I'm just like you are. I'm no different than you people."

But one of the jurors saw me differently, and she said so. "No, Mr. Foster. You're not like us. You're too influential in this community, and we're going to do something about you."

When she said that, I knew it was a witch-hunt. And there I was before them, being grilled on phases of my business, and the line of questioning seemed absurd. It appeared that their minds were made up already, and it wouldn't have mattered what I said, they were just going through motions here. I knew I was going to be indicted, I just didn't know what for. And I felt, by looking at the faces of the other eleven jurors, that she was speaking for all them. It was a frightful group to depend on for justice, having heard their petty questions and all this accusation, which as near as I could tell was for being successful in life. I couldn't imagine any juror ever speaking in such ways to another citizen upon whose fate they had the power to decide. But it happened to me, and I just took it. There could be no reply. What could I say? Nothing. And this could happen to anyone in America.

I didn't have to speak before the grand jury. I did have the right to declare the fifth amendment, like Mark Furman or O.J. Simpson, but to me, to declare the fifth would be to declare guilt. We didn't feel we were guilty of anything, and we didn't have anything to hide, so we chose not to hide behind the fifth amendment. Our attorneys advised us we had this right, and one of them advised us we should do it, because in his thinking, if we didn't say anything, there would be absolutely no way for them to use our own words against us, like they later were able to do with Jeff.

I found out what I was indicted for just the same way that the public found out: through the media. After appearing before the grand jury, I got out and went home and had told my wife, "Let's go out of town. I just need to get away from it all. I've had all I can stand, especially today. You won't believe what that was all about."

So we went to Saratoga in the motorhome to spend the night and hopefully play golf the next day. But going to Saratoga didn't get me away from it. At ten o'clock that night on the Cheyenne Channel Five News, I got the information that I had been indicted for blackmail. I also found out at the same time that my daughter had been indicted for blackmail also, and that my son had been indicted for blackmail and price fixing.

When I heard the word which had been so viciously alleged at me and my family, it called to mind the most ugly images, images of gangsters breaking people's legs, phone calls and threats and thugs and money, bad money, extortion, dirty little secrets and sex affairs and dirty sex. To see these images in my mind, of what blackmail meant to the average person, and think about the grand jury accusing me of blackmail, made me wonder, made me shudder at the thought, that the public would now think of me as some sort of thug, and wonder who I had beat up, and who I had maliciously used or abused or threatened. It was unbelievable that there could be such an allegation. It now appeared that they were trying to smear me, to make me look as bad as possible to the public. The fact that they had the power to do this behind their secret little protected veil was a realization that drained me. The blood drained from my head and I must have looked ghostlike. I now knew that my life was out of control, my public image was out of control. This made me feel a very deep depression. Tension and stress set in. My stomach knotted up, and it would turn out to be a long time before I would get a good night's sleep. In the public mind, I was now another person, a person I didn't even know.

When I saw our place of business, Foster's Country Corner, on TV, and the description of myself and family as blackmailers and price fixers, it is impossible for me to describe the despair I felt. For many days, and many nights, I couldn't lie down for more than five minutes without having to get up and move around. I was desperate to keep my sanity, had to continually find things to do. I couldn't help a feeling of hate which began to build inside of me. And that hatred continued to build and get even worse. I went on with life, as people have to do, but not as the same person inside. This experience changed me. And again, I reflected back on my life, and the principles I had chosen to live by, and especially my decision about sobriety, and hoped that these would all survive. And I also had to reflect on the changes I had made in my life because I had quit drinking, and hoped with the higher power for strength to not let this hate destroy my life. This seemed the strongest temptation for me to drink and try to forget my problems since that day in 1956 when I decided to quit. But I was able to think about what I'd learned in Alcoholics Anonymous, and remember Step One: I'm powerless over alcohol. I knew if I started drinking that the situation would only get worse and I would have no control over how to fight this situation and that would be just what they would like to see.

So, after the grand jury had written their indictments and had been dissolved, in part to keep my sanity, I lashed out. I sent a letter to each and every one of the grand jury members at their homes. All their names were on the first page of the court record which the clerk had copied for me. So I wrote a letter, and sent it to all of them.

December 7th, 1983
Pearl Harbor Day

To Albany County Grand Jurer[sic]

Enclosed are several reports you had in front of you that show Lies, Malicious statements by the Sheriff's department and accusations in the Branding Iron that you knew were false, yet You used this material to prosecute me and my family. You let the County Attorney lead you around by the nose even though you knew much of what he was saying were lies, just so you could write indictments against me and my family - WHY!!! - Do You have no honor or do You just hate me and my family that much. In any case I believe you need to look at yourself in the mirror every morning and ask yourself if you like what you see.

Respectfully,

Dick Foster

Because of the date and comment "Pearl Harbor Day," I heard through rumors, the jurors had tried to turn this letter into a threat of violence as if they were to be bombed. Of course it was no threat. Fortunately I had also written, "in the mirror every morning" proving this. Obviously I had no intention of in any way interfering with their hopefully long and healthy lives. I was merely indicating reference to their consciences. They had let the prosecuting attorney lead them around by their noses, and based on public records given to me by the clerk at the county court house, the following appearances were disclosed:

COMPELLING CIVIC INTEREST

On Behalf of the State of Wyoming:

Richard E. Dixon, Esq.
Deputy County and Prosecuting Attorney

Karen H. Maurer
County and Prosecuting Attorney

Grand Jurors:

Lawrence M. Ostresh, Jr.

Phyllis Baxter

Caren Collins

Becky Davis

August Deibert

Barbara Jensen

Anthony Papa

Ronald Reher

Scott Smithson

Collette Theis

Marion Varman

Sandy Wasmuth

CHAPTER FOUR

My son and daughter had also been called in to testify before the grand jury, and Jeff, especially, when he came back, said they hardly asked and hardly talked about price fixing, but about suppliers, where we bought, and why, and how. As it turned out, this had laid the groundwork for Jeff to be later set up for an indictment, with, if you can believe it, the milkman, who would suddenly come to see Jeff for no apparent reason. It seemed obvious that the county attorney had determined that price fixing against me wasn't going to fly. So now they were on a desperate hunt to save their public images and waste of public money.

As I mentioned earlier, the county attorney had indicted Rex Guice on seven counts of price fixing, ahead of the grand jury efforts. What I didn't know was that they had offered him immunity on those charges if he would testify against me before the grand jury to the affect of accusing me of this. So my fate, in part, now rested on Rex Guice's integrity. Rex had refused the immunity, refused to lie about me price fixing, and therefore I was never charged with price fixing at the county level. I would have to say at this point that Rex, and his wife, Betty, would not sell their soul for personal gain. They refused the temptation offered by Richard Dixon to lie to save themselves. When I found out they had this opportunity to lie and didn't, it reaffirmed my faith in humanity and human honesty and in them. His principles were more important than gain. And as I found out later, these charges could not have stood up in court anyway because they lacked the element of a complaining witness, an essential element for prosecution of price fixing, a misdemeanor. At least this was my understanding.

My son Jeff had been charged with price fixing, but Judge Hanscum had thrown out the indictment for lack of a complaining witness at the outset of the trial. This made me believe that the indictments against Rex Guice had been illegal from the beginning, because to my knowledge there had never been a complaining witness in any of this gasoline investigation. So they had simply used the indictments to smear Rex and the industry, knowing they could have never prosecuted him. Of course, Rex probably hadn't known this at the time, and neither did I until charges were dropped against Jeff, who had also been smeared.

But through the milkman's testimony, the county attorney was able to create the elements of blackmail against Jeff. In order to have blackmail, you have to disturb someone's property, he has to have suffered bodily harm or mental illnesses, his livelihood has to be threatened, and it takes these elements to constitute blackmail, which was the furthest thing from my mind, because the situation between our company and the milkman was impossible for me to imagine in these terms. It turned out that the sole sentence of incrimination by my son Jeff, had been his statement, which he didn't deny the wording of, to the words he spoke to Gordon Dubard, who was the milk wholesaler from whom we bought for years, to whom Jeff had said, "If you don't trade with us, we're not going to trade with you."

They were able to take this sentence to mean blackmail, as if Jeff had threatened him in some way. To me and to Jeff, this simply meant that we were free to buy milk where we wanted, just as he was free to buy gas where he wanted. But there was more, there was false testimony from another gas dealer by the name of Roy Purdy, who owned the Chevron dealership on Third Street in Laramie. This was the man that the sheriff's department worked with to try to get indictments for price fixing, and it was Mr. Purdy who had said in front of the grand jury, that I, Dick Foster, personally appeared in his gas station to try to get him to raise the price of gas. This was a complete lie, and I knew that Roy Purdy knew that I wasn't ever in his gas station, but he told the grand jury what they wanted to hear, and they pressed him, as I could surmise from the testimony, to use my name. The milkman, it turned out, had been buying his gas at the Chevron station from Roy Purdy. And when Jeff found out Roy Purdy had given false statements to *The Branding Iron* against us, and that the milkman was buying gas from him, Jeff had decided to tell the milkman to go ahead and sell his milk there, too. I think Jeff's feelings had been hurt. And thus, the statement had been made by Jeff to the milkman, "If you don't trade with us, then we're not going to trade with you." Jeff's statement had been precipitated by the actions of the grand jury and by Roy Purdy's false testimony to them, and now was being used by the grand jury to indict Jeff for blackmail.

Before Jeff appeared before the grand jury, Gordon Dubard (the milkman) had come into Jeff's office and had asked Jeff, "Are you saying that if you see one of our trucks in Roy Purdy's service station, that you will stop trading with me?"

And Jeff had said, "Yes, that's what I would do."

Well, it was a natural enough reaction by Jeff, considering that Roy Purdy had lied to the grand jury and Jeff knew it, and for the milkman to buy gas there seemed an insult, and Jeff thought he had the right to buy his milk wherever and from whomever he chose. But Jeff had unwittingly said something which had been interpreted not as Jeff's freedom to buy where he wanted, but as a threat to the milkman.

The milkman had apparently been instructed by someone to come and talk to Jeff, and see if he would say something which could be used in this manner. The milkman had apparently been advised as well. I mean, he came to get something, and from the looks of things to me it seemed he knew what needed to be said by Jeff to get a blackmail charge initiated. I believe the man who consulted with the milkman was the sheriff, Donald Fritzen, whose wife, I had heard, was an employee of the milkman. This sequence of events, the calling of the grand jury, the subsequent visit of the milkman to Jeff's office, and the charge being filed against him, had all the elements of a sting type operation

51

bordering on entrapment. When the milkman got on the stand, he told the grand jury what Jeff had told him, and that this had caused his back to ache, his body was hurting, and it became a mental problem for which he had to seek guidance from his preacher at church, to help him get through this mental stress which had been inflicted upon him. And in order to have the elements of blackmail, he had to be able to say on the stand that he was mentally disturbed by this, and he had been threatened with his livelihood, which caused his whole body to ache and become ill because of these circumstances. This all had to be said or they couldn't have brought the charge.

The picture of Gordon Dubard going into this sad state of life and business as a result of Jeff's telling him what he asked to hear, and came on his own volition to solicit, made me rather ill and dispossessed. My gosh, this was the same fellow who a few months before all this grand jury business began, had come to me trying to peddle his whole milk business to me, saying he wanted to get out of it. I had said no, we didn't want to get into the milk business. And now, he had become the prime witness for the sheriff's department and the grand jury to get the elements they need to create the blackmail charge, and hopefully in their minds, save this whole grand jury business from becoming a complete public farce. It appeared that the only "crime" which the grand jury had discovered, was one that had been created either just before or just after they were formed. And my son Jeff, was the scapegoat.

Jeff had come back from a two-year mission for the LDS Church, and upon presentation with the charge against him, it was immediately apparent to me that Jeff didn't even know what blackmail was, much less be capable of it. So he'd been easy to set up. And the milkman had been so desperate that I think he would have done anything to get out of the milk business. I've always questioned in my mind, if he really felt this way about our company, why did he go to Jeff, who had only been working in the company for a few months, instead of coming to me? He would have known that such policies would have to be approved by me before ever being initiated. So it became apparent that they had targeted someone with little business experience within my company, which happened to be my son, and they used him to the fullest to fulfill their need so that they could get some endictment through the grand jury.

To add to the irony of the milkman and his story, I couldn't believe what I had heard five days after the trial, that he had suddenly been hired as a deputy sheriff by Donald Fritzen, the sheriff whose wife had worked for him. Further, it made me wonder if Dubard had even been required to take a physical for the job. This is a man who had just said he was disturbed, had to see his preacher for mental guidance, and his body ached. I couldn't understand how the sheriff could determine this man fit for the job. Of course, there is a strange ring to it all, the way it began with his trying to sell his floundering milk business to me, and how it ended with his job in the sheriff's department. It made me wonder if any of the other witnesses the sheriff groomed would later get on his payroll.

Of course, the way all this looked against Jeff during the trial was very different from the picture drawn here and now, after the events, now that the inner-connectedness of the people and their little rewards have come to be known by me. Looking back, I can see how they all did it and pulled it off. To save themselves from the farce they had created.

Another indictment had also been written against Wayne Swain, who had been a long-time employee of mine, and also had the authority to buy and purchase for the stores. He had been indicted for allegedly blackmailing the potato chip man. Apparently, Richard Dixon thought he was my son-in-law, and I don't believe he would have ever gotten indicted if Dixon had known he wasn't family. That charge went to full-blown trial after which a jury acquitted Mr. Swain after a five-minute deliberation. Obviously, the jury felt, as I did, that the charges were absurd.

But my son, Jeff, got indicted and so did my daughter, Trudy, as well as myself. My attorney had been contacted and told that we could come and appear on our own, without being arrested and "brought in" by an officer, that we should come down immediately to be fingerprinted and officially charged in person. No bond had been required; the judge had spoken to the fact that we lived there and were well established and not likely to go anywhere.

So we all went together to the courthouse and went to the sheriff's department who does the fingerprinting, and an officer by the name of Ide had the privilege of fingerprinting me and my two children. And I could see without any question in my mind that Ide was enjoying his job to the fullest. I can't explain the feeling of a broken heart while I watched him actually laugh as he took the fingers of my daughter and son and pressed them into the ink and rolled them onto paper.

Because there were two indictments against Jeff, there was a question of whether Jeff needed to be fingerprinted again. The judge had told my lawyer that no, this would not be necessary, and that information had been passed along to Jeff. But Officer Leazenby, in his zeal for the case, called Jeff anyway and told him to get his ass in there or he was going to come out personally and get him.

The humiliation from that time on became unbearable, and sleep continued to be a stranger in my life.

CHAPTER FIVE

Along with the county grand jury investigation, one other investigation had been instigated by the Albany County Sheriff's Office in conjunction with the County Attorney's Office: the FBI. This agency had come after me behind the lines; I was only peripherally dealt with in this regard. The typical black-shoe agents did not come directly to me and harass me, or any of my family, but they worked hard and diligently to pore through seven years of my business and tax records, searching for some indication of wrongdoing.

We received court orders to box this information up and send it to Washington DC for analysis. If I had been the least bit crooked, I would be in prison today. Also, I believe they had tapped my telephones for some time, as well as those of the other oil jobbers in Laramie. This had probably stemmed from the original Leazenby report, which said that the FBI might be interested in this as well. It was as if the sheriff's department had brought in as many guns as they could to smoke me. Their zeal made this an incredible ordeal for me and my family. They made such a thorough investigation that even a needle in a haystack would have been discovered. Of course, it was all in vain.

After the FBI had reviewed and scrutinized all my records, another grand jury appearance was demanded of me! This time, a federal grand jury. The federal grand jury is always in place, ready to act, and in this case, located in Cheyenne, Wyoming. I received notice to appear, as did all the other dealers who were being investigated along with me. Rex Guice was one of those who had to appear before the federal grand jury, and he later told me that this jury, just like the county grand jury, had offered him immunity if he would testify to incriminate me.

The federal grand jury had twelve members, and it was a much more pleasant situation to have to appear before. They were more professional and actually looking for a crime; it was not their intent to create one. So after they questioned me, and finished their investigation, they exonerated me. I didn't like being accused in all this, and the double jeopardy of the federal as well as county grand juries bothered me, but at least they were civil enough to exonerate me. This felt good, because when you've been looked through with the thoroughness of the FBI, believe me, it's all hanging out. And I was proud that my business and personal activities had come out perfectly clean. There was only one question that they asked me that I felt had credence to their investigation, but it was a question I couldn't answer. They asked me about a twenty minute long-distance phone call from my office to the Mini-Mart office in Casper, Wyoming, another company with numerous gas stations throughout the state. Their direct question was, "Who do you know in the Mini-Mart office in Casper?"

And I truthfully told them that I knew no one in that office. But they then asked me again, "Mr. Foster, who do you know in the Mini-Mart office?"

"I know no one in the Mini-Mart office."

And for the third time, the U.S. attorney leading the grand jury, said to me, "Mr. Foster, I want you to know you are under oath, and if you do not tell us who you know in that Mini-Mart office, it will be perjury. So I will ask you one more time, who do you know in the Mini-Mart office?"

I then looked at that gentleman and said to him, "You can ask me this question twenty-five thousand times, and I still won't know anybody in the Mini-Mart office."

And as I go back over this conversation and the appearance before the federal grand jury, after I was dismissed from the stand and mulling it over in my mind on the way back to Laramie, it became apparent to me that the only thing those people had in question about me and my business was, who did I know in the Mini-Mart office in Casper? And I can understand why they wanted to know that, because Mini-Mart had three stations in Laramie and they were trying to tie me with price fixing with Mini-Mart in Laramie. That had been the last question they asked me, and then they had dismissed me from the stand.

This was different from the county grand jury, in that when the county investigated me and found nothing, they pursued an alleged new crime against Jeff by using the milkman's testimony, which looked to me like a set-up. And my alleged crime as a result of this apparent set-up was "accessory to the fact," a conspiracy charge, also a felony, meaning that their last straw against me on this whole trumped up affair was to try and prove that I told Jeff to blackmail the milkman. So they had to convict Jeff first because without his conviction, no crime had been committed and therefore no conspiracy could have caused it.

But to see the Albany County Grand Jury find a crime in the discussion between the milkman and Jeff, which they so hienously labeled blackmail, just because their investigation showed me and my family to be clear of any misdoing in their grandstanding in the news about price fixing and kickbacks and all this supposed gasoline crime, made me burn even hotter inside. Because now I began to realize that it was they who were committing a wrong against me and my family and ultimately, therefore, against the people of Laramie themselves. Because there had been no price fixing, as had been alleged, and gas pricing in Laramie had always been fair, but the people of Laramie had been led to believe that they had been cheated for years, and that my success and that of others had been at the expense and cheating of the people in Laramie, the same people who once elected me to represent them on the City Council for four years.

So the magnitude of the affair increased, not only in its long-term implications against me, but in its long-term implications for the City of Laramie, or even the whole system of law under which we all operate. The sheriff's department, the county attorney's office, and the district judge are all implicated. As this thought occured to me, I began to look at the situation somewhat differently. The shock of being publicly accused and ridiculed and disgraced had been hard to live with and accept, knowing I was innocent, but now to know that I had been accused by people in such respectable postions, like a judge? A deputy county attorney? A handful of sheriff's officers? A grand jury? This frightened me, because I still had to go to trial along with my son, Jeff, and these people had alleged what they were calling blackmail, and we faced felony charges, which was quite serious for two men who had never been in any kind of trouble like this, and thought they never would be in their whole lives. So what purpose did these people have in mind with this, I had to ask myself.

This got into a logic problem. First, the judge is supposed to be impartial in a proceeding or investigation, if anything, his first duty is to protect the innocent. We have a system whereby you are presumed innocent until proven guilty. But this is the judge who participated in the formation of the grand jury, in his letter declaring it in "public interest." But the letter said nothing about a crime having been committed. So perhaps from the beginning, the pupose of the grand jury had been bastardized from its design to discover crime, into a design of what the judge called, "public interest."

So now, I got the strange and absolutely scary feeling that to these people, it was in the public interest that I be found to have committed a crime. Now think about how that made me feel. Here I was, trying to show everything about my life, for all these people to see, and saying to them, "Hey, I'm innocent. Look! I have nothing to hide. Here are my records. Go for it. There's nothing to this."

But the response I was getting, over and over again, was, "No, Mr. Foster, you're not like us. You're too influential in the community and we're going to do something about you." This statement rang deeper and deeper into this, and really began to haunt me. It was morbid. It was insane! It was unimaginable! Why me?

This realization of the way the judge and county attorney and a few sheriff's officers seemed to me to be setting me up made me wonder at what basis any of them had in the very beginning to launch this attack. So as I prepared for trial, these thoughts were not firm yet in understanding, they were just a feeling, kind of like the feeling one gets of foreboding, like the thoughts are not words yet, but there's something tangible building, because the search in the mind for understanding is almost constant when you're in a situation like this. It takes over your whole life. And it certainly had control of mine, and even raised questions to me about what it meant to be in America, and to have this huge system, which in all its parts, is designed to keep conspiracies among agencies from happening. The sheriff doesn't work for the judge. Neither does the county attorney. These safeguards in the system came into question to me, and I went to trial with Jeff with both eyes open, I guess ready for anything now. I had been shocked over and over again by the insane accusations and creations of some of these people, and now I had to face them in a trial of several days of looking at them and them at me, and listening, and watching for innuendos which might help me understand what was really going on here.

All in all, there had been seventeen indictments, and all these charges of supposed crimes, price fixing, perjury, kickbacks, and conspiracy by several others besides us, all these charges had been dropped but one, against Wayne Swain, and that hadn't held up at trial. The only two people remaining to go to trial were me, Dick Foster, and my son, Jeff. He was labeled with blackmail, and I was labeled with conspiracy to blackmail. It was the only thing the county grand jury had left, the only possible conviction which could save their faces in the eyes of Laramie, Wyoming. It had all come to this, to this thing that they were calling blackmail, to this thing they had set up with the milkman, to this thing Jeff had said to him when he came into our office out of the blue, right? When he came in and solicited the comment from Jeff which in its entirety was, "If you're gonna buy your gas down there, sell your milk down there." In essence, if you don't trade with us, we're not gonna trade with you. And I was accused of telling Jeff to tell that to the milkman, as if I knew ahead of time that the grand jury or somebody was going to tell the milkman to come into our office, as if I knew ahead of time that out of the blue, here would come the milkman, into our offices, not to sell milk, but to ask of Jeff, not me of course, but to ask Jeff, "If you see one of our trucks down at that Chevron station, are you going to stop buying milk from me?" I had been accused of planning all of the above. Well, I knew I didn't plan it, and I knew Jeff didn't plan it, but when we went to trial, it became fairly self-evident that somebody had.

This brought to mind all the bankers I've talked with over the years while trying to get a loan. They have asked repeatedly if I had my bank accounts with them, and have said that if I did it would make it a lot easier to get the loan. This is the same as saying, if you don't bank with us, we're not going to give you a loan.

But the burden on me now did not allow me to pursue the wrongdoings of those who had come after me, because my hands were tied. And I was having to deal with all this newspaper and television coverage condemning me.

Even my mother. She was living in Laramie and had lived there practically all her life, from early childhood on. And, of course, I was the talk of the town, and front-page news, and so she knew all about the accusations. My brother, Bob, informed me one day of a conversation he'd had with our mother. He told that he had come out and ask her if she thought I was guilty of these crimes, and she had told him, "Yes, because they wouldn't do what they're doing to him if there wasn't some truth in it."

This crushed me. Now, this is the mother that raised me. That taught me right from wrong. That taught me to respect the law. And to be respectful to those who enforce the law, because they have a hard job. And as I thought about what she had taught us, I could see that she believed in it herself, beyond any personal feelings she may have had to the contrary. Because she felt that all enforcement officers had principle and honor, the same as she had taught all of us kids to have in our younger years under her supervision. She always had said, "Dick, respect the law, and those who enforce it." This belief in her was so deep she wouldn't overcome it for anyone. To her, if the sheriff accused someone of a crime, it would be with good reason.

So I was defenseless here, because I could never undo the fact that I had been indicted by this grand jury in her eyes. And as I thought about it further, I wondered what I would now tell my children about all this, and decided that I would have to say, "Respect the law but watch those who enforce it, because wearing a badge does not guarantee their honesty or integrity. And God help the man that the bad cops come after."

My mother died shortly thereafter, so I have to just carry this grief within me. After she died, there had been a scrapbook of pictures of my childhood and whole career which my mother had kept, so I knew that my mother had been proud of me and of my achievements from this, and other indications, but one thing seemed held back: the articles she had clipped from the newspapers about the grand jury and accusations against me. These articles were in there, but in a separate envelope, and not pasted in the scrapbook with the rest of my life, as something separate, which didn't fit. And from the remark she had made to Bob, I had the feeling that she may have gone to her grave still feeling I may have been guilty of these crimes merely on the fact that the deputy county attorney had done what he did; her belief in authority was that strong. She had been a great influence in my life, helping me understand my drinking problem, and when I finally made the decision to quit drinking and go to Alcoholics Anonomous, she was a great factor in my ability to do this and I had maintained sobriety since that time. Because of her complete support, she had made it easier for me to overcome the problem. She had even joined Al Anon, to work with and help anyone she could to overcome their drinking problems, which in my mind is an addiction more than a disease. That had been the last time I had really needed her to help me with a problem. And that had been a long time ago, June 20, 1956. And now, it really disturbed me that these allegations had struck so deep into her heart, and mine, and again, I was powerless to change this, because her feelings and respect for the law and those in it were so deep in her heart that it wouldn't matter what I would say. Nothing could change this.

So while the sadness of this sank in, I guess I had to realize that to other people, I must have looked guilty too, even though I hadn't even gone to trial yet. If the press had been so convincing to my own mother, I had to think about how convincing it must have been to everyone who read it. I mean, they made it look like they really had me, like I was really the guilty rat. And with this the way it had happened, I had to undertake some very unpleasant steps, I had to do what was responsible, and one of those things was to voluntarily resign from one very prestigious position which I held in Laramie at the time: I was on the Board of Directors of what was at that time Citizen's Bank of Laramie, now known as Bank of Laramie. I had been one of the ten founders of that bank, and had served two years as a director.

In addition to my own feelings on this, I suddenly got a letter from the State Banking Examiner, Mr. Bonham, informing me that state law empowered his office to ask me, if they so desired, to resign from the board of directors of the bank. This would be done if they felt it necessary to protect the bank and its depositors. This letter had been sent because of the endictment against me alleging blackmail, which was a felony, notwithstanding that I had not been convicted of anything.

After due consideration, and seeing possible liability against the bank because of the publicity I was getting, I made the decision to resign. I didn't feel it would be fair to the other directors or to the bank itself to be dragged into this mess which had me trapped.

There was another aspect which triggered this action to resign. Another strand of the web which had accused me was connected to the bank: Barbara Dubard worked for the bank. I might add that she had been a very good employee at what she did. But she was married to George Dubard, the son of Gordon

Dubard, the milkman who had accused Jeff of blackmail, and information was leaking from the grand jury that they were concerned about her well being in her job. Even though my relationship with her had been good, and there was no way I would have ever interfered with her job, this was still a factor in my decision to resign, because I didn't even want the possibility of another accusation, and I didn't want the possibility of any of this to cause harm to Barbara. So on July 8, 1983, I wrote a letter to the bank resigning my position. This is what I wrote:

It is my understanding that you have some concerns as to the well-being of Citizens Bank because of indictments that were recently handed down by the Albany Grand Jury and signed by the Albany County Prosecutor. You should also understand that a present employee of Citizens Bank is a spouse of the person listed by the county attorney as a witness supporting the charge of the indictments. I have reasons to believe that there is some concern that my position on the board of directors may have been discussed before the grand jury as to the welfare of the participating employee that I mentioned. If I was not on the board of directors at Citizens Bank it would seem apparent that I could not adversely affect the welfare of the bank or the employee I have mentioned. I have lived in Laramie all of my life and one of the last things I wish to do is harm anyone. I do not believe that I am guilty of the crime that is, in my opinion, maliciously charged against me. Based upon the facts and reasons I have written, it is with great regret and personal concern that I resign from the board of the directors of the Citizen's Bank on June 30, 1983.

By now, I guess as much damage had been done publicly to me as could have been done prior to the trial. I was actually looking forward to the trial, because it would be regular jurors and I would be allowed legal counsel, which I wasn't in the grand jury proceeding. And I hoped that the trial jury would not have some secret agenda. At least my attorney would have some say in jury selection, and there was always the hope that it would be a fair trial and that justice would prevail.

I was desperate for information which could explain how I had been implicated so heavily in this grand jury investigation, it had seemed to me from the very beginning that someone was after me, more than anyone else in the business, and I just couldn't figure out why, or what I had ever done in this community to deserve this scrutiny. I wondered if maybe it was the result of all the charitable things I'd done, my high visibility in the community. I didn't know, but wanted to find out.

So I asked my attorney what I could do, and he suggested hiring a private investigator, which we did, as I recall his name was Richard Miller from Cheyenne, and we hired him and he went to work to try to find out what was going on.

Miller did not, to my knowledge, ever discover the Leazenby kickback report, but he did discover something related to Leazenby. He reported to us, among other things, that there had been a meeting held in the sheriff's office in the Albany County Court House, and several officers had been present, and the report stated that Leazenby had said, "Let me go out and see Dooley. I will get what we need." At the time this hadn't meant much to me, and apparently my attorney felt it not necessary to depose Leazenby and get to the bottom of this. So we simply let it go, not realizing at the time that this had resulted in the Leazenby Dooley kickback report.

CHAPTER SIX

The trial of Jeff for blackmail and price fixing, and me for conspiracy, began in conjunction with the trial of my daughter, Trudy, who had been charged with blackmailing another supplier, the bread man, Art Morgan, who had also been called before the grand jury. The details of the charges brought against Trudy were similar to those against Jeff, but the breadman had apparently said, "It's apparent to me what you're looking for, and I'm just not going to be able to help you." But they brought the charges against her anyway. So the trial began with a closed-door jury selection process. Over one hundred people had been called and given instructions to be there so they could evaluate them one-by-one and pick the twelve who would sit in judgment. This took three or four days, and as I remember probably eighty of the hundred people came before Deputy County Attorney Richard Dixon and my attorney. I got to see all this, and could begin to see how the selection process works. Each attorney asks questions of the juror being considered, and both attorneys agree or disagree on whether to accept or reject the prospective juror. Each attorney is allowed so many rejections without cause. I think it was twenty each. Rejections with cause resulted from discussions between the attorneys, and by mutual consent, some were rejected.

One thing I couldn't help but notice during this jury selection was that anyone who came before the prosecuting attorney who was in business for themselves in any way, shape, or form, was automatically rejected by him without cause. There were no business people who made the jury, in my recollection. I thought the prosecuting attorney did this because anyone who had some business experience could have seen that the freedom to choose one's suppliers was essential in any business. And that when they saw what this trial was about, any business person could see how easily it could be set up for anyone in business.

The selection process continued until there were twelve jurors. I had known who a couple of them were but didn't know any of them personally. It was about an even mix of men and women. The men wore coats and ties and the women wore dresses.

So the trial was called to order, there sat the twelve jurors, and the presiding judge was the Honorable Arthur T. Hanscum, unbeknownst to me at the time, the same judge who relied upon the Leazenby kickback report to call the grand jury. As I look back, I can see that this was the last chance to save face for all of them, the whole bunch who had brought this mess, and there he sat at the top of the pile, in black robe and mustache.

As the trial opened and they got into the discussion and testimony it became evident that there was a problem with Trudy's indictment. So my attorney and the prosecuting attorney, and Judge Hanscum called a side bar, where the three go to the side of the courtroom where no one else can hear and discuss the problems at hand. After this first side bar, my attorney came back to our table, and the judge immediately dismissed the charges against Trudy. In my opinion, the reason the judge had to do this was because they didn't have the elements necessary for the charge of blackmail to begin with. I believe this was because the breadman had refused get on the stand and claim that things Trudy had told him had caused his back to hurt, and caused fear of his livelihood, and perhaps caused him to be driven to his preacher to get his mental faculties back. In other words, the breadman in my opinion had refused any suggestion by the prosecuting attorney to say that Trudy had caused all this damage to him by something she supposedly said. And because of this, they had no leg to stand with her charge of blackmail. And also because of this, I think the breadman is a proud man, and was honest, and could see that the county attorney would have to humiliate him as a bread dealer, in order to convict Trudy as a blackmailer. The glove didn't fit the breadman, and I was glad to see that he was a real man, and stood up to this for his own integrity.

So Trudy was out of it from the start, and no longer had to sit at the table with Jeff and me. Now she sat back as a spectator. We were glad for her, and of course wished that the same thing could happen with the milkman.

As it turned out, the milkman was the sole witness against us, the only one the prosecutor could use, the only one called to the stand to testify as to Jeff's blackmail and my conspiracy.

When the milkman was called to the stand, he walked up to the stand, and I couldn't see any back problems in the way he walked, in fact, he looked perfectly normal to me. Even though he claimed mental stress and strain, his mental thoughts and spoken words about how he had been blackmailed were remarkably clear, as was his recall of his back problems and stress, and meeting with the preacher, this was all perfectly clear in his mind, as was the final element: that Jeff had caused all this with that one statement.

Of course, no one had brought up the issue of why he had come to see Jeff all of a sudden, or why he had asked only one, very specific question of Jeff, and why he had elicited one specific response which he seemed to have memorized, and that was, "If you see one of my trucks in the Purdy Chevron Station, will you quit trading with me?"

And now, as the prosecutor brought it out, I understood the full import of why it had to be asked so perfectly. It couldn't have held up if it had been just, "If I buy my gas there, will you cut me off," it had to be, "If you see my truck there..."

Now the reason for this, as it suddenly turned out in the trial, was, Jeff just seeing his truck there didn't mean Jeff knew he was buying gas, he may have been getting a tire repaired, or a lube job, which are services we don't offer. So the impeaching content against Jeff was the utterance by Jeff as interpreted by the prosecutor, to the effect that Jeff would stop buying his milk even though he may have not been buying gas from Roy Purdy at the Chevron station. This was the trap for Jeff when he took the stand. It seemed that Jeff's statement to the milkman would not have been illegal if Jeff had simply implied that the milkman should buy gas from us rather than Purdy, since we were buying his milk. But the way the prosecuting attorney was presenting it, Jeff's statement restricted the milkman from buying anything from Purdy's station, including services we don't offer. So this was why it was so critical that the milkman had to present the trap just right to Jeff, and had to have the exact words of "if you see one of my trucks there," which meant that seeing a truck there did not prove the purchase of gas. Therefore, Jeff had unwittingly been duped into the element they needed to create blackmail.

As all this unfolded in front of me, as I looked at this milkman from whom we had purchased milk for our stores and restaurants for five years or more, and heard how all this had been perpetrated against Jeff, I recognized how perfectly it had to have been orchestrated.

And now, here it was, and I realized that this had happened after the grand jury, that Jeff had been upset, as I had been, because Roy Purdy had lied to the grand jury about me having been in his service station, and then along came the milkman, preying on Jeff's anger at Roy Purdy, and preying on that anger, had trapped Jeff into responding to one carefully crafted sentence.

They would never have pulled this off against me. I would have kept my anger in check, even if the milkman had suddenly presented himself as a vent for my anger at being lied about by Roy Purdy. But Jeff didn't have the experience in life that I had, and had been goaded into saying something, which what he said was not incriminating in itself, Jeff's words were not enough to incriminate him, it had been his response of "yes" to the milkman's tricky sentence.

Jeff had come off a two year mission serving the Lord and the LDS Church, and the furthest thing from his mind was the meaning the prosecuting attorney was assigning to this conversation between Jeff and the milkman.

Now there was never any further questioning of the milkman, and the most critical aspect of his testimony, which in my mind was, why did he suddenly come to Jeff with all this?

So this went the wayside to the court. My attorney had chosen not to cross-examine the milkman, and in one stroke of a hand, and one quick statement, he declined cross-examination and the milkman stepped down, unscathed. I couldn't do anything right there at the table, I just had to watch this man walk away as I still sat there with Jeff.

In the next recess I asked my attorney, somewhat still in shock, why he had refused to question the milkman, and he had said, "Let the jury decide. They're not stupid. They can see through this man. Anybody would know you didn't have to go see your preacher for a cause such as this."

But there was one thing he hadn't thought of, which as it turned out, would be our undoing: the judge's instructions to the jury.

Now when Jeff took the stand, if he had chosen to lie, even just a little bit, they could have never made the trap work to convict him. But he was so honest, that when he was asked questions, he said yes, just like he had to the milkman. So they led him along and he never lied and told the truth and it came down to that one sentence and the question to him, had he responded yes? And he aswered that he had. And that was that.

As I think back on it, I'm only more proud of my son for being so honest in the face of such ridicule, in the face of people who were obviously taking advantage of his honesty and even naivete, but that's the way the legal system worked in this trial, and take advantage of him they did. But I'm proud that he didn't bend his own integrity. I hoped that the jurors would recognize this in him, and compare his integrity to that of the milkman, and as it turned out they apparently had, except for one crucial factor: the judge and his instructions to them.

Now when I took the stand, I was asked all the same stupid questions, and the one question they were driving at was to try to set me up to say that I had told Jeff to say that to the milkman. And it was the milkman himself who had asked Jeff the question which caused this. It wasn't until the judge's instructions were given to the jury that I realized that he had put those instructions in such a way that Jeff would be convicted if they followed his instructions. And further, they had to convict Jeff in order to convict me. If Jeff was not convicted, there was no conspiracy, so there could be no conviction against me.

So there it was, if you don't nail the kid, you can't nail the old man. Well, they nailed the kid.

But ironically, the jury had seen that I could not have possibly conspired to create the events which the milkman described. So they acquitted me.

Ironically, also, after the jury had been sent to deliberate our fate, and my son and I had gone to the restroom in the Albany County Court House, in the City of Laramie, I told my son, "Jeff, the judge's instructions, if followed by the jury, were given in such a manner that you stand a good possibility of being convicted. There is also a good possibility that I won't be convicted. Because no one was able to set me up. Not the sheriff, not the county attorney."

81

Here is instruction number three:

The defendant, JEFF D. FOSTER, has been charged with an offense declared by statute to be contrary to the laws of the State of Wyoming. The charge was made by what is called an indictment, as follows:

That JEFF D. FOSTER, late of the county aforesaid, on or about the twenty-eighth day of March, in the year of Our Lord One Thousand Nine Hundred and Eighty-Three, at the County of Albany in the State of Wyoming, committed the offense of "blackmail" in that said Defendant, at said time and place, did threaten to do injury to the property of another with intent to compel the person threatened to do an act against his will, to wit: did threaten to injure Gordon DuBard's livelihood unless DuBard ceased doing any business with Roy Purdy, which act was against DuBard's will, the same being in violation of Wyoming Statutes S6-7-601 (1977) and against the peace and dignity of the State of Wyoming.
> Given:
> Arthur T. Hanscum
> District Court Judge

The judge, right here, defined Jeff's statement to stop buying milk from DuBard as a crime, ignoring Jeff's intent, which was to sever all ties with Roy Purdy. Purdy had made false statements to the press about me and Jeff knew it and was simply trying to keep his distance from Purdy, and didn't want to have any common suppliers with him. There was no intent to blackmail DuBard, or to commit a crime. If you don't have intent, how can you commit a crime?

Further, this instruction declared that DuBard's milk route was property which Jeff had threatened to destroy. What property did he have in our business? Well, where is Jeff's right to quit doing business with a supplier if he wishes to?

Our attorney tried to get Judge Hanscum to add instructions to the effect of what I've mentioned here, but the judge refused. I still can't believe this was allowed to go to the jury. It sealed Jeff's fate. At this point, I felt the judge became the jury.

Here is instruction number four:

The Defendant, DICK DEWANE FOSTER, has been charged with an offense declared by statute to be contrary to the laws of the State of Wyoming. The charge was made by what is called an indictment, as follows:

That DICK DEWANE FOSTER, late of the county aforesaid, on or about the thirtieth day of March, in the year of Our Lord One Thousand Nine Hundred and Eighty-Three, at the County of Albany in the State of Wyoming, committed the offense of "accessory before the fact" in that said Defendant, at said time and place, did aid or abet in the commission of the felony of blackmail, which felony is in violation of Wyoming Statutes S6-7-601 (1977), to wit: did aid and abet Jeff D. Foster in committing the crime of blackmail against Gordon DuBard by reinforcing the object of said blackmail demands and as well, reinforcing the threat used to force DuBard into acquiescence, the same being in violation of Wyoming Statutes S6-1-114 (1977) and against the peace and dignity of the State of Wyoming.

Given:
Arthur T. Hanscum
District Court Judge

83

Even though this instruction says the offense is "accessory before the fact," all testimony shown and put into evidence during the grand jury proceedings, and all conversations I ever had which were brought into this trial were "after the fact" and the grand jury knew this, and still wrote this indictment. I can only assume that they believed that a jury would convict me as well as Jeff even if my knowledge of Jeff's statement was after the fact. They didn't take into consideration that a real trial is not conducted in secret like their proceedings, and this aspect couldn't be hidden at a regular trial.

Sadly, I believe these charges were brought against us because the deputy county attorney who was leading the grand jury in a dog and pony show had found nothing to prove gasoline price fixing in Laramie, so to try and save face he trumped up these blackmail charges over why and from whom we would purchase milk!

Instruction number five:

The Court instructs the jury that the Indictments filed in these cases against the Defendants are mere accusations of charges and are not in themselves any evidence of the guilt of the Defendants; and no juror in this case should permit himself or herself to be, to any extent, influenced against the Defendants because or on account of the Indictments filed in this case.

Given:
Arthur T. Hanscum
Judge

This is a great one. Hanscum says the indictments are not evidence, yet it is the definition of the law explained in the indictments which directs the jury in what evidence would constitute guilt. The indictments are clear in saying that a statement by Jeff to stop buying milk from Dubard constitutes a crime, ignoring the issue of freedom in business to select one's suppliers, but most importantly, the indictments presume an intent on Jeff's part which is as far from the truth as possible.

We must examine this issue of intent as it pertains to Jeff's actions, because his intent and motive for what he said was never *examined* in the trial. It was only *presented* in the criminal definitions brought forward in the form of indictments and judge's instructions to the jury, and in the words of the prosecutor during the trial.

Exploring Jeff's intent is the real key to understanding the preposterous nature of the indictments and the trial. As I see it, it was the presumption by the grand jurors that we, the Fosters, were greedy, and to feed our greed, we were fixing the price of gasoline, and we were trying to force people in the community to buy gas from us, rather than at other stations. They failed to find evidence of price fixing, so that issue died with the grand jury. But convinced of our guilt and greed, convinced of this to the degree that they felt us capable of such a terrible crime as blackmail to achieve our evil ends, they construed Jeff's intent of the statement to DuBard as greed-motivated, as an attempt by Jeff to force DuBard to buy Foster gasoline. There was little doubt that in Jeff's mind since we buy DuBard's milk, he should buy our gas. But that does not mean that if he wouldn't do so, Jeff would threaten to stop buying his milk, that there was any evidence of an intent to force him against his will. But the way the judge's instructions went, motive had nothing to do with guilt.

This was totally wrong. Jeff's real motive never came out in the trial, or even as an issue in the trial, a terrible injustice within the proceeding. Jeff's motive was this:

Other suppliers that we bought from had come into our office after being at Roy Purdy's station and they told us before the indictments came out against us, that we were going to be indicted, and that they heard this from Purdy at his station! Well naturally, we didn't want to hear this. The grand jury proceedings were supposed to be secret. So Jeff had felt that he didn't want common suppliers with Roy Purdy. He didn't want to hear any more of these rumors. So when Gordon DuBard came around Jeff expressed this desire to DuBard, as much as a *courtesy* as anything. He could have simply cut DuBard off and started buying milk from another milk supplier, but he meant no harm to DuBard, he simply didn't want any connections to Purdy. So rather than cut DuBard off cold, he told him how he felt, and told him if he saw his truck at Purdy's station he would then stop buying his milk. This was not intended as a threat, it was said to inform him in hopes that DuBard would understand and that they could continue doing business. There was never intent to do harm to DuBard, Jeff didn't want to stop buying his milk, Jeff simply wanted to stop the rumor pipeline which flowed out of Purdy's station via suppliers. The statement was not a threat, and it certainly had no basis in greed for DuBard's gasoline business.

But Jeff's statement was construed differently at the trial. The prosecutor grilled Jeff into acknowledging that the statement was an *ultimatum*. Threat had been too harsh of a word for Jeff to accept, but *ultimatum*? Jeff agreed, yes, his statement was an ultimatum. By agreeing that his statement had been an ultimatum, Jeff had been construed as agreeing that he'd made a threat, intended to do harm to DuBard, and intended to commit blackmail. None of this was his true intent or motivation. What Jeff meant was for him to choose who he wanted to do business with, either Purdy or us, and then Jeff would do the same, and pick who we want to buy milk from. So the basis of the statement was not to manipulate or threaten or injure DuBard, but to let him know that we simply didn't want any business connections at all with Purdy. To call this blackmail in the form of an indictment was absurd in my mind. And the judge's instructions to the jury strengthened the words of the indictments, and took away the jury's real task, to choose the word or words which truly described Jeff's intent. Which word should they think about, *threat, ultimatum, statement, inform*? I've written this book to let the reader decide which word should be chosen.

Instruction number six uses the word *threaten*:

Pertinent portions of the Wyoming statutes provide as follows:

Whoever, either verbally or by any letter or writing or any written or printed communication, demands of any person with menaces of personal injury, any chattel, money or other valuable security; or whoever accuses or threatens to accuse, or knowingly sends or delivers any letter or writing or any written or printed communication, with or without a name subscribed thereto, or signed with a fictitious name, or with any letter, mark or designation, accusing or threatening to accuse any person of any crime punishable by law; or of any immoral conduct, which, if true, would tend to degrade and disgrace such person, or in any way to subject him to the ridicule or contempt of society; or to do any injury to the person or property of anyone, with intent to extort or gain from such person any chattel, money or valuable security, or any pecuniary advantage whatsoever; or with any intent to compel the person threatened to do any act against his will, is guilty of blackmailing.

Given:
Arthur T. Hanscum
District Judge

Here the logic is that Jeff must have threatened, and also either was trying to force DuBard to do something against his will (not trade with Purdy), or was threatening to damage DuBard's property (stop buying milk). A blackmail charge is serious stuff! It conjures up the idea of forcing someone to do something against their will, like trying to force them to commit a crime, or beat someone up, or pay money by threatening to expose them. And when I think of a threat of damage to property, I think of a threat to blow up someone's house or car, or violence. Nothing even resembling this applied to Jeff's intent with his statement. And the law clearly requires "intent" of some sort.

It is instruction number eight which attempts to drag me into this:

Pertinent portions of the Wyoming statutes provide as follows:

Every person who shall aid and abet in the commission of any felony, or who shall counsel, encourage, hire, command, or otherwise procure such felony to be committed, shall be deemed an accessory before the fact, and may be indicted, informed against, tried and convicted in the same manner as if he were a principal, and either before or after the principal offended is convicted or indicted or informed against; and upon such conviction he shall suffer the same punishment and penalties as are prescribed by law for the punishment of the principal.

In this case, you may not find DICK DEWANE FOSTER guilty of aiding and abetting JEFF D. FOSTER in the commission of the crime of blackmail unless you find JEFF D. FOSTER guilty of blackmail.

GIVEN:
Arthur T. Hanscum
District Judge

Obviously, if they didn't convict Jeff, then no felony had been proven, and therefore no conspiracy. So this made it clear to the jury that if they wanted to convict me, they had to convict Jeff as a prerequisite. I have always felt that the parties involved felt that if they could make this stick on Jeff, that they were sure to get me on the conspiracy charge. Fortunately they were wrong about this; even with all these instructions, the jury just couldn't go that far. But I also feel that the motive for trying to convict Jeff was the issue of gasoline prices in town, and sick as it is, a conviction against Jeff for this milk statement must in their minds have represented a move toward better gas prices in town, and further, at least some result from all the grand jury and trial expense. I believe the prosecutor felt that these motives would ultimately win him a conviction against both of us, no matter how flimsy or absurd his case on blackmailing the milkman was. This feeling of mine goes back to the original letter by Judge Hanscum citing a "compelling civic interest" for forming the grand jury rather than investigating a crime. And now it appeared that "compelling civic interest" had not only concocted the crime (notably after the formation of the grand jury), but created the guilt in my son as well.

Instruction number nine went further into my charge:

The necessary elements of aiding and abetting the felony charged are:

1. The crime occurred within the County of Albany on or about the date of March 28, 1983; and

2. The crime of blackmail was committed by someone as a principal; and

3. The Defendant knowingly and willfully aided and abetted, counseled, encouraged or otherwise procured the commission of the felony, the elements of which are set forth in another instruction.

If you find from your consideration of all the evidence that each of these elements has not been proved beyond a reasonable doubt, then you should find the Defendant not guilty.

If, on the other hand, you find from your consideration of all the evidence that each of these elements has been proved beyond a reasonable doubt, then you should find the Defendant guilty.

GIVEN:
ARTHUR T. HANSCUM
District Court Judge

Note the words, "knowingly ... procured the commission of a felony."

Instruction number ten required the jury to "assume that each defendant is innocent unless you are convinced beyond a reasonable doubt and from all the evidence in the case that he is guilty." And further, "if you have a reasonable doubt as to the truth of any of the elements of the crime, you should find the defendants not guilty. If you have no reasonable doubt as to the truth of any of them you should find the defendants guilty."

At least instruction number ten gave us that, but then the judge went on with further instructions to "define" the elements of a "threat," and other aspects of the case. Note the absolute requirement of a threat in instruction number eleven:

A threat is defined to be a menace of such a nature as to unsettle the mind of the person on whom it is to operate and take away from his acts that free, voluntary action, which, alone, constitutes consent. Any clear language would be sufficient to convey the threat, but no precise or particular words are necessary. You must find that there was the actual communication of a threat from the Defendant to the threatened party.

The threat must also be received in such circumstances that a reasonable likelihood of "alarm" or "fear to his discomfort" be raised in the threatened party.

GIVEN:
Arthur T. Hanscum
District Court Judge

Is Jeff's statement what you would think of as a "menace of such a nature"? Would Jeff's statement create alarm or fear in a normal person? The jurors here were instructed to accept the judge's definition of a threat, even though Jeff would not admit intending it as a threat. DuBard said he had gone to his preacher to talk about his unsettled mind, indicating the degree of menace and fear with which he had wrestled. Of course, he would have had to do something like go to a preacher to appear to be convincing, in my opinion. It was my lawyer's opinion that we needn't cross-examine DuBard because his claims were so absurd that it should have been obvious to the jury. But the judge's instructions continued to give credence to DeBard's receipt of an actual threat and his resulting frightened state of mind. It amazed me that he was hired within five days after the trial as a deputy sheriff. If Jeff had scared him, how would you like to have to depend upon DuBard to protect you in his capacity as a deputy against a real threat?

The instructions went on in number twelve on this:

In order for you to find that Defendant JEFF D. FOSTER committed blackmail, you must find beyond a reasonable doubt that the alleged threat in itself, or as affected by attendant circumstances, would reasonably be regarded as capable of moving an ordinarily firm and prudent person to comply with the blackmail demand.

GIVEN:

Arthur T. Hanscum

DISTRICT JUDGE

DuBard, this "ordinarily firm and prudent person" never did comply with the so-called threat. And we never quit doing business with him until after the trials, at which time DuBard, as I mentioned, became a deputy under the sheriff who had investigated the matter.

The final definition concluded the matter by defining property as the jurors were instructed to understand it, in instruction number thirteen:

In order for you to find that Defendant JEFF D. FOSTER committed blackmail, you must find beyond a reasonable doubt that he threatened to do injury to the property of the DuBards. In this context, property is defined to include any advantageous business relationship which the Dubards had the right to own, possess, enjoy, or dispose of.

> GIVEN
> Arthur T. Hanscum
> DISTRICT JUDGE

This, in my opinion, capped the well of hope for the jury to see this any way but how the judge wanted them to see the case. Having defined threat, he now defined property as including "any advantageous business relationship which the DuBards had the right to own, possess, enjoy, or dispose of." So now, the jury had been instructed, as I read this to mean, that Gordon DuBard had a *right* to own our milk business. And further, that only he had the *right* to dispose of it. So now, my purchase of milk from a supplier is a property owned by my supplier, and only they may dispose of it? I think not. Heaven forbid, this would mean that any time you indicated to a supplier that you might stop buying from him, that you were blackmailing him. This is a felony, here, what we're talking about. So here was the threat, here was the injury, and here was the property that Jeff had threatened to injure.

With this defined this way to the jury, I think they threw common sense to the wind, because, because mind you, I think they felt they had to obey the judge's instructions, and his instructions defined blackmail in such a way as to define Jeff's guilt for them.

One instruction regarding my guilt, which the jury in my opinion also followed, was one which I think *saved* me. Look at instruction number fourteen:

A person aids and abets the commission of a crime if he knowingly and with criminal intent aids, promotes, encourages, or instigates the commission by act or advice.

GIVEN:
Arthur T. Hanscum
District Court Judge

95

The words "knowingly and with criminal intent" I think saved me. I think the jury saw how absurd it would be to think that I knowingly and with criminal intent aided, promoted, encouraged, or instigated Jeff's statement to the milkman. The absurdity of the whole matter flares up in me as I write this. They could not have believed that Jeff had any criminal intent of blackmail, either. But intent was not gone into on his part. And the judge's instructions, one of which I think saved me, I think totally did him in. In the strange way that language sometimes creates reality, they had goaded him into saying on the stand that he'd given an ultimatum, which they then defined to the jury as a threat, and a fearful one at that, and then carried their definitions all the way to even define property.

As irony reached its fullest moon on this several years later, by chance, one of the jurors made a remark to my son-in-law, who had become his friend later due to other circumstances, that it was only because of the judge's instructions that the jury found Jeff guilty. They felt they had no choice. And then I understood why several jurors wiped tears from their eyes as they emerged from the deliberation with their verdict. It's too bad that the recent publicity regarding the right of jurors to ignore judge's instructions had not come sooner so that this jury would have known they had the right to decide in spite of what the judge had basically ordered them to do by definition.

So the verdict of guilty for Jeff had been read to the court, and also the verdict of not-guilty for me. So while I stood exonerated, I had to watch my son walk up and stand in front of the judge and listen to instructions about when and how they would sentence him. I really can't describe this feeling I had as I watched, but I watched. At least I had the pride that I had also watched my son be honest in the face of all this acrimony, and knew in my heart that the only criminals in this room were those who had accused us. And even though it was extremely adverse conditions which had brought us together there that day, I realized that my pride and love for him would never change, and I realized also that I had known him well all along, and that his integrity was something I believed he would always keep. In fact, I couldn't help but say it to myself in these exact, bitter words. "I knew he had more principles in his little finger than they had in their whole bodies." For some reason this sentence has stayed with me to this day, as if I had been forced to create one to equal the creation of the sentence uttered to my son by the milkman.

The sentencing had been set for several days later, and the people who appeared at the sentencing, the deputy county attorney who prosecuted the case, Richard Dixon, my wife,

Dorothy, myself, and of course the judge, Arthur T. Hanscum.

Beyond my belief, the county attorney, who has a considerable amount of input as to the degree of punishment which my son should be forced to endure, had said, "This boy came from a good family." And then recommended leniency by the court. I instantly wondered what he would have said if I had been convicted also, because their whole purpose of this whole thing had gone the wayside when they failed to convict me. It was me they had wanted and come after and tried to set up, and now all they had was Jeff, my son.

Then at the sentencing we were asked by the judge if there was anything we wanted to say before he made the sentence. And through the tears of my wife, as she had been crying quite heavily, she had said somehow, I mean she couldn't speak, but she indicated no, there was nothing she had to say.

And then the question was directed at me, personally. And I said, "Yes, I do have just one thing to say. This boy has more principles than anybody in this room. And to be convicted of blackmail is an absurdity in my mind." And as I think back on that statement, I probably wouldn't have said it. Because here I had told them that my son was better than them, and this might have aggravated them. At least I had the decency to modify what I said away from the original and everlasting version which I really thought. I still had respect for the law and the court enough to be civil and polite.

So the judge ordered a preliminary background check on Jeff before actual sentencing to make sure that there were no other charges or convictions against him in his life to help them determine what the degree of sentencing should be. As I knew it would be, of course, they found nothing incriminating in his past.

And after this last delay, the sentence was handed down: Jeff was sentenced to a probation period, after which time if he successfully served his probation, the charge and conviction of blackmail would be expunged from his record, meaning, that he would no longer be the felon they had made him out to be, and there would be no record of this ever having occurred.

In my mind, this was all unbelievable, that for a whole year, all of our lives in my family had been like tits in a ringer, with them jumping up and down on the handle. Again, I could see that some of the people who were administering the system hadn't been very happy convicting my son instead of me. As unscrupulous as Jeff's conviction had been, at least they had stopped it right there, and not sent him to prison, and not forced him to carry the burden of this conviction on his record in the future. Now, by doing this they had eliminated any need for us to appeal this conviction because in six months it wouldn't exist in public record anyway. Of course, if they hadn't stopped it right here the way they did, we would have appealed the case to the Wyoming Supreme Court. I believe they would have overturned the conviction. I still can't conceive that our milk business is someone else's property, and I'm sure that the seven supreme court judges would see it that way too. It is possible that the judge and county attorney had thought of this, and by expunging Jeff's record they would keep the case from going any further.

CHAPTER SEVEN

So, with the trial over, it seemed the shock of it all would begin to wear off and life would return to some semblance of normalcy, or at least ease back into what it had been before. I didn't want to harbor any ill feelings over this, and forgiveness seemed foremost on my mind. I had to struggle with this because I felt I had been wronged, and was mulling it over, feeling rather sullen about it all.

And then one day, as chance would have it, I happened to see Rex as I was standing on a piece of property I owned which was next door to and bordered the property of his service station. Rex and I said, "Hello," to one another and speaking casually, he mentioned laughingly a reference to all of the sheriff's reports which had been generated throughout the investigation. He asked me if I had seen them all, and how did I like the Leazenby kickback report?

I didn't understand his humor, and told him that, well, I thought I had seen everything that our attorney was supposed to have, everything they had done to accuse us, and then added, "Kickback report? No, I don't believe I ever saw that one."

He said, "Would you like to have a copy of it? I've got it."

"I sure would. In fact, I'd like a copy of all the sheriff's reports you've got."

So he made a copy of them and called me and we met in the restaurant out there. And for the first time, I saw the Leazenby and Dooley kickback report, which I couldn't believe when I saw it. As I read it there, right in front of Rex Guice, the shock of what I read cast me into a whole different frame of mind. And I sat there aghast at the knowledge that I had never been allowed to see this during the prosecution, and wondered why Rex had been privileged to see it when I hadn't, and neither had my attorney. I must reprint this here for the shock of its force to be read again, as I read it that day for the first time.

[EXHIBIT A]

ALBANY COUNTY SHERIFF'S DEPARTMENT

SUPPLEMENTAL REPORT: C# 83-0583 PAGE: one

DATE OF REPORT: 3-22-83   OFFICER:Leazenby 520

On 3-21-83 at approximately 1215 hours I contacted Kevin Dooley, the owner of the Outrider truck stop in Laramie. This contact was made in the loby[sic] of the truck stop. At this time Dooley and myself had a conversation about the price fixing investigation that is being conducted by the Albany County Sheriff's Office.

At this time Dooley was not advised of his rights, as no questions were asked of him concerning this investigation. Dooley advised me that he knew that there was an investigation taking place, and also advised that he was aware that price fixing took place in Laramie. Dooley advised me that he was not envolved[sic] because he sold very little gas, most of his business was selling diesel fuel.

Dooley stated that he knew about the price-fixing and also had information as to who was envolved[sic]. However he would not divulge this information to me. He did state that if he was ever placed under oath or summoned as a witness that he would tell the truth, but at this time he did not want to tell me about it.

He did state that Rex Guice was not the one that we wanted, that there were other people that were more or less forcing him into this. He stated that he had information that Dick Foster was forcing Guice into paying him (Foster) a one cent kick-back on every gallon of gas that was sold at Guice's stations. Dooley would not elaborate on this

103

except to state that he (Dooley) had also been approached in the distant past about paying a one cent a gallon "fee" for every gallon that he sold so that he (Dooley) would not be under sold. He would not tell me who approached him on this, but I had the impression that it was Dick Foster.

Dooley stated that the way he arrived at his gas prices was to watch the rest of the stations and stay with them on the prices.

At the end of this conversation I advised Dooley that there was a possibility that a Grand Jury might be called to investigate this, or that there was a possibility that the Feds might be interested in it. I advised him that if this took place it was strong possibility that every station owner in Laramie would be called to give evidence in the matter. Dooley advised that he was aware of this, and if it happened he would have no other choice but to tell the truth.

At this point the conversation was ended.

Leazenby   520

This was basically the end of my conversation with Rex that day and my mind was in a whirl. The question kept rising in my mind, why hadn't I seen this when Rex had? And with a little bit of thought, anyone could figure out, as I had surmised, Rex had been given that report because Richard Dixon knew he was going to offer immunity to Rex, and they wanted Rex to think that the sheriff's office had proof that I was receiving a one cent per gallon kickback for every gallon of gas Rex sold, and further that they could prove other dealers were also giving me a one cent per gallon kickback. So Richard Dixon, in effect, had attempted to coerce Rex into testifying against me, by trying to show Rex that they already had proof against him and me. But they would offer him immunity if he would testify against me to the effect that we had price fixed, and about the kickbacks.

So you can imagine the pressure on Rex to lie. To Rex, they had given the appearance that we'd both already been had and that the sheriff's office could prove it. So if Rex would only substantiate this, they would let him go to get me.

Rex stuck to the truth, and even with the request of his attorney, John Scott, who had also been told Rex would get immunity if he would testify against me, Rex stood stalwart on his ground and told John Scott that there was no way he could do this, because it simply had not happened.

105

All this ran through my mind with regard to Rex, and then my thoughts returned to the substance of the Leazenby and Dooley kickback report itself. Now according to this report, Dooley was saying that Rex was being forced into paying me a kickback. This was so specific and strong against me, and Rex of course, but to read this about what I was supposedly doing, and to remember the trial and that neither Leazenby nor Dooley had testified against me, and to think that Judge Hanscum and Richard Dixon had called a grand jury on the basis of this, and indicted me and Jeff and Trudy, and attempted to prosecute us on the basis of this report, which never surfaced at trial, and these people never said under oath anything about it, or anything at all, for that matter, this made me steam! And as I thought further, I realized that the grand jurors had also seen this report, and were willing to indict me and my family, and that these people were not ever going to testify. I felt that they all knew or should have known this kickback report was false, was contrived. At least they could have given me the chance to rebut it. All of them knew, the judge, the prosecutor, the grand jurors, they all knew! They had to know!

If the trial jurors had seen that this report started all this, and then saw that Dooley and Leazenby would not testify, they would have known that this whole grand jury scheme, and all

106

the indictments were false from the beginning. No wonder none of the indictments had held up. No wonder nobody ever got prosecuted for price fixing, or anything, except us, for the so-called blackmail charges which had been concocted and set up just like the Leazenby report had been used to set up the grand jury.

The weight of this on my mind was an incredible burden. Because now I realized that there had been a malicious and intentional conspiracy at the sheriff's office, in conjunction with Richard Dixon, the deputy county attorney, to present enough information to Judge Hanscum to entice him to call a grand jury. I could not believe that the judge would have believed this about me, and I wondered why the judge did not ask the sheriff's department to verify this information, to at least get something under oath, some real statements, at least interview Rex Guice. This report was nothing more than rumor. Dooley didn't say that he saw kickbacks being paid, he had said only that he had information. Well, what information? None of this was substantiated. Why not?

The more I got into this, the more it didn't fit. My curiosity continued to build, and my wish to forgive began to deteriorate. It was one thing to be falsely accused and tried, it was another thing for people in power to abuse their power, and the system, especially if those people lied and conspired. I felt I had to have some answers, here. This threw the whole power structure of Laramie into question, at least the whole legal system at the county level. This was not a pleasant thing to think about, much less try to do anything about.

When I carried these thoughts to their fullest implications, I realized that to find out the real story, I was going to have to take all these people on. And that seemed an incredible task, and that brought to mind all kinds of possibilities of what might happen to me in process. After all, they had already shown what they could and would do to a person unjustly, and believe me, I had been through plenty as a result of what they had done, and I wondered what else they could think of to do to me if I started digging into this.

But I felt a duty here, to myself, to my family, to Laramie, for that matter. I felt a duty which I couldn't turn my back on. To turn my back would have been to accept something I now had good reason to believe was wrong against me and the whole system under which we all live. And I felt that the people in power should be bound to live by the same rules of honesty and integrity and law that we, the common people, are bound to live by. Perhaps, as my mother would have thought, they were bound to an even higher standard. Well, I was beginning to uncover a very low standard, perhaps even an illegal conspiracy, and once I got started, and felt this duty, I committed myself to a goal to find out what I could, whatever the cost, whatever the risk. I recalled something one of my old supervisors had told me when I was a manager of a Standard station in Centerville, California, now known as Fremont, his name was Mr. Blout, and he had said, "Dick, if you're ever going to progress in your responsibility as a manager and in life, there are two things you need to do. One, take nothing for granted. And two, accept nothing but the best."

So with the decision I'd made to get the real story of the grand jury, I thought through some of the implications of this decision. And what I would have to do to achieve the truth in the actions of what some very powerful people had done. And also, what these people, still in power, might possibly do to me to hide what perhaps, should have been public record all along.

With these thoughts, it occured to me that the easiest way for them to set me up again would be to plant some drugs on me, or my premises, and then prosecute me for that. They'd have a better chance of getting me with that kind of set up, because the drug laws are so strong, if they could just plant some evidence, which seemed easy enough if they had some. So to counter this possibility, or at least get the jump on it, I took my son-in-law,

Warren, the attorney, to an audience with the City of Laramie Chief of Police, Jerry Overman. And I told him in advance that this was a concern to mc and that I wanted it on record that if it happened, that I've come to you and wanted you to know that this was a possibility.

He had responded, "Oh, Dick, there isn't anybody here that would do that to you."

And I told him that I didn't have the full confidence that he did, and that I felt compelled to bring this possibility to his direct attention. I certainly couldn't go to the sheriff's department with it. And at a later date, after all this was over, at an activity which had been held at the convention center at the Foster's Country Corner, I had the opportunity to speak with Mr. Overman again, who had attended that event, and who had since retired as chief of police and had run for the office of clerk of the district court and won, and now worked daily in the Albany County Courthouse building, and he had said, "You know Dick, that was probably a good move you made when you came and talked with me about the possibility of the planting of drugs at one of your businesses." And I asked him to elaborate on this for me, but he didn't say anything further. So I assumed that he had become aware, as I had, of such things as the Leazenby and Dooley kickback report, and possibly of other things I didn't know about. But he wouldn't have talked about this any further, which I understood, because he was a man of integrity and always had been to my knowledge. And if the city police department had been involved in the price fixing investigation, I don't believe anyone in his department would have done anything like what the sheriff's department had done with Leazenby and the report.

So having at least covered this base as best I could, I now set out to get to the bottom of what had been done to me and my family, to find out how it had even been possible, and to find who had been involved in it.

At first glance, there was now John Leazenby, sheriff badge number 520, along with Officer Fanning, and Donald Fritzen, the number one man, the elected sheriff. These were the people who immediately came into question in the sheriff's department, because they had to be part of the investigation to produce the Leazenby report and deliver it to Richard Dixon, the deputy county attorney. There was no way Leazenby could have taken this report to Richard Dixon without approval of Donald Fritzen, and possibly that of Fanning, oddly enough, the brother-in-law of Donald Fritzen! To top this off, it turned out that Fritzen had two sons who were also on the payroll as deputy sheriff's officers. This looked like a lot of nepotism to me, and I

111

wondered who else might be on his payroll in either that or some form of favoritism. And as I thought of the officer who fingerprinted me and my children, Officer Ide, I remember the look on his face as he smirked at us and held our fingers in ink, and it now seemed obvious to me that he knew about the whole set up and was getting quite a thrill watching us suffer because of the power they had wielded against us.

So I needed to know more about these sheriff's office people, and about their actions, as well as the county attorney's office and Richard Dixon, and the judge, Arthur T. Hanscum. Other names, I was sure, would surface as I got into this, and I prepared myself for as long a drag out as the one they had put me through, and I wondered how many of them would come out of my investigation as clean as I had come out of theirs. Quite frankly, I felt the number would be small.

One thing came to mind as I began the investigation which needs to be mentioned here. I knew that some of these people had targeted to get me, and only me, from the word go. I knew this because the sheriff's office had never come to us and ask us any questions at all about the allegations of price fixing and who might be doing it and how it might be happening. They never ask us anything, but they ask everybody else in the business, to see what they could get on us.

I discovered that the very first effort to prove price fixing in the valley was by Dick Schroeder, a commissioned agent under contract with Asamara Oil Company to sell their product and the gas was given to him on consignment, which he sold through a Gasamat station in Laramie on South Third Street, and he only paid for the gas after the sale. As I found out later, he had been slow in paying Asamara as agreed for the gas. The fact was, Asamara was preparing to eject him from the station, and Dick Schroeder filed suit against Asamara Oil Company as a result of their attempts to remove him. So I went to the court house and discovered documents confirming the existence of the lawsuit against Asamara which he had initiated.

The Gasamat had been one of the stations which Rex Guice had visited in person to ask them (Dick Schroeder & Company) to take a survey of the gasoline prices in Laramie, because Rex knew that Dick did not have the authority to change the price at the pump for the gas. Asamara held the right to set price because they still owned the gas at the time of sale. So Rex had hoped Dick would look around Laramie and gather the information as to what other dealers were charging, and then pass this information on to Asamara's offices in Denver. From that information, Rex had hoped that Asamara would respond to market conditions in Laramie, as reported, hopefully, by Dick

Schroeder. So this was the basis for the "survey" which Rex had encouraged. So it wasn't that Rex had conspired to set price, Rex had simply asked Schroeder, another dealer, to take market information for himself and send it to Asamara for their consideration.

Schroeder had not been at the station at the time that Rex came by to see him. So Rex had left a message there asking that Dick give him a call.

So Dick Schroeder placed the phone call to Rex Guice, and had his telephone recorder ready, because he taped this phone call without Rex's knowledge. This had been an illegal act to start with, because you are required by law to tell someone if you are taping the conversation over a phone call. But Rex hadn't been advised he was being recorded.

Rex, in that conversation, asked Dick to take a survey, and Dick Schroeder asked Rex why he was making this request. Rex informed him that some prices were going up in Laramie, and that he would like to see him take a survey of competitor's prices so he could send it to Asamara's offices. In the tape, the only person that Dick Schroeder mentioned was me, Dick Foster, and he asked Rex, "What has Foster done?"

And Rex advised him that he should go out on the street and look at the price sign, and he would know what Foster had done, but Rex said he thought I'd gone up.

This was basically all there was to the merits of this conversation, and the typed transcript had never been given to me for me to see how my name had gotten involved.

As I looked into this situation, I found out that Dick Schroeder had Albany County Sheriff's credentials at this time and had been working for them, at least on a part-time basis. And it became my belief that Schroeder had been in conversation with Donald Fritzen, the sheriff, and that they had made a decision to target me before this phone call was even made to Rex Guice. So I think that Dick Schroeder had purposefully, as a sheriff's deputy, mentioned my name over the phone to Rex, in order to implicate me. Now I had been in Hawaii when this happened, but when I found out that Schroeder had been a sheriff's deputy but had made the call to Rex under the cover of his identity as another gas dealer, I could only conclude that Rex had been set up, too, and specifically to get something on Rex in order to manipulate him to try to get something on me.

And after this phone call, the sheriff's department immediately went around to all the other stations similar to Gasamat, those stations where price control was decided at corporate offices out of town, to see if Rex had contacted any of them. It came to pass that he had, and Rex had asked them to

115

perform surveys just as he had asked Schroeder at Gasamat. It is my belief that at this point, the sheriff's department took the information they had gathered on this to the county attorney's office, and sold them on the idea of a major investigation on price fixing of gasoline in Laramie. A decision was made and two deputies were sent out to arrest Rex Guice: John Leazenby and Glen Bennett.

These two deputies are the same ones who had gone out to Kevin Dooley's station, and it was one of them, Leazenby, who had said at the sheriff's meeting that he could go out and see Dooley and get what they needed for a grand jury. Ironically, I found out that Leazenby at that time was a part-time employee of Dooley's! Leazenby had been driving trucks for Dooley and pulling fuel from the refinery for Dooley Oil Company. So when I found this out, and then read the Leazenby report, it made sense to me that Leazenby had worded the report in such a way that Dooley was off the hook right then from any allegations of price fixing. Of course, Leazenby's quote that Dooley was mostly selling diesel fuel and not gasoline was ludicrous. The fact that I also sold diesel had been of no merit in my case. But this had been very clever, that Leazenby could quote Dooley as accusing me of taking kickbacks, but quoted Dooley as saying he wouldn't mention any other names, but if he was put under oath, would tell the truth.

Now bear in mind that the other sheriff's deputy who went out there with Leazenby, was Glen Bennett, and Deputy Bennett had been in charge of the price fixing investigation, and for some strange reason, Bennett had stood off the side while Leazenby spoke with Dooley, and had not personally heard any of the supposed conversation which resulted in the Leazenby report. This would later turn out to be very important, and again, very clever, because there had been no witnesses to the conversation and what had been said. How strange, that the lead deputy, the head of the investigation, had stood off in a corner and let Leazenby conduct the questioning alone. this is especially strange because Leazenby had a vested interest in Dooley's well-being and "innocence," it would be obvious that Dooley's employee would not be the appropriate deputy to question him, unless of course, Leazenby could use his relationship with Dooley to some special purpose, as I believe he darn well did.

So we now have the only two tangible pieces of evidence, the taped conversation and the Leazenby report, both generated by sheriff's deputies who also work directly in the gasoline business. Talk about an inside job! Schroeder and Leazenby. So how well would that evidence hold up to my scrutiny, and how would those two men hold up to my scrutiny?

So I set out to find out about these two, and starting with Schroeder, found that he had once been the chief of police in Hanna, Wyoming. And that the Hanna City Council had called him in front of them and for reasons only known by them, asked him to quit using the city's police car for anything but official business. They were trying to cut some costs. This I was able to document by the Hanna City Council Minutes of the meeting. When Schroeder was confronted with this, he immediately resigned from the Hanna Police Department. As I recall, one or two other men working under him resigned also. The council immediately accepted his resignation. Schroeder then moved away from Hanna. Perhaps there had been other issues involved, but I wasn't able to substantiate them. But one thing was clear to me from this, his personal interests outweighed the public interest in terms of how he would conduct himself in the line of law-enforcement duty.

I then found out that he had gone into the printing business with a partner. Suddenly, his partner had been arrested and convicted of the huge and heinous crime of counterfeiting! Who could believe counterfeiting in Wyoming? But it happened, and Schroeder's partner pleaded guilty. Schroeder was never charged. Schroeder had said that he hadn't known his partner had been using the equipment which they owned and operated together, to copy paper money, I think it was twenty dollar bills. This I was able to confirm through a newspaper article reporting on the conviction.

I believe it was after this that he then went to the town of Rock River, which is in Albany County, and near Laramie, and became the Albany County Sheriff's Deputy serving in the Rock River area. Suddenly, there had been a rumor, and I don't want to give a rumor too much credence, but I will mention it as only such, but the rumor was widespread about how it was impossible to drive Highway 30 through Rock River without getting a speeding ticket. Anyway, he hadn't been a sheriff's deputy too long there before he came to Laramie and became the commissioned agent to sell gasoline for Asamara Oil Company, which is also known as Gasamat, the name under which this business operated. So I found out that he had Albany County Sheriff's Office credentials to be a deputy.

So not only did Dick Schroeder have an interest in the sheriff's department of Albany County, he had an interest in his lawsuit against Asamara, when he taped the conversation with Rex Guice. But as I had discovered, and as I will show later, nothing these people did ever got followed up on or prosecuted, or ever get any headlines in the newspaper, or even seemed to matter to anyone. I guess if you are a deputy, or former deputy, you can break the law without recourse, and you can set others up as criminals as you so desire, even if you have to break the law yourself to do it. And as I watched other trials, and saw what other police had done, I began to feel that America was losing it, because time and time again, the police were breaking the law to get their supposed "criminals." Policemen throughout the nation were getting caught saying things like, "I can do anything! I'm a police officer!" And this wasn't just happening in LA either. Waco. Ruby Ridge. It goes on and on. And all I could do was finish my investigation of how it happened in the small city of Laramie, Wyoming, and hopefully do something about what I found.

On Leazenby, I don't want to go into that, primarily because the facts and circumstances surrounding the Leazenby and Dooley kickback report itself were enough to make Sherlock Holmes roll over in his grave. When I saw that Leazenby worked for Dooley, that just flabbergasted me.

So all in all, I knew what I've described here, and the fact that nothing held up against Rex Guice or ever came of the Dick Schroeder matter, and the fact that neither Leazenby nor Dooley had testified in my criminal trial as to the kickback allegation, showed me that there was something fishy about this report beyond the obvious contrived nature. It occured to me that there could only be one reason why they didn't testify: they knew, both of them, Leazenby and Dooley, that the allegations were false.

The only way I could force this issue into public scrutiny was to file a civil lawsuit naming Leazenby and the sheriff's department for slander and libel and defaming me. Only in this way could I force them to testify under oath and publicly answer to me and the community as to this report and why and how it had come to be.

So the suit was filed, and I now hoped I would have some justice, at least be able to clear my name once and for all and be free of this duty and burden which I felt.

CHAPTER EIGHT

I retained the same attorney who had defended me in the criminal proceedings to develop and file the civil suit against Leazenby and the sheriff's department. I had wanted to sue the deputy county attorney, Richard Dixon, also, and in conjunction with the sheriff's department because of John Leazenby, but it had been my attorney's advice that we leave the deputy county attorney out of it, because there would be a good chance that he would quickly be dismissed from the case because he would be immune from liability for his acts as deputy county attorney.

So the decision was made to sue only the Albany County Sheriff's Department and John Leazenby (only in his capacity as deputy, not personally). We knew that there was no way for the Leazenby kickback report to be put into the hands of the county attorney without the express approval by Donald Fritzen, the elected sheriff, so it was the department that we named in the suit.

I had shown the Leazenby and Dooley kickback report to my attorney, and just as I had been, he had been astonished. He had not seen it until I brought a copy to him, and told me that it had been improper procedure for this not to have been shared with him in my defense during the criminal trial. So my rights had been abridged, and this had been illegally kept from me and my attorney. It was with reluctance that my attorney took on the job of this civil suit, feeling that the difficulty of prosecuting the sheriff or county attorney or judge, for that matter, would be great and that there was little likelihood that they would be forced to be accountable for their actions, whatever they were. So the decision was made to sue only the sheriff's department, and we would use the deputy county attorney, Richard Dixon, only as a witness whom we would subpoena to the stand to confirm the use of this report, to prove that it had been used in their decisions to prosecute me.

We then also felt the need for a different judge from Arthur T. Hanscum to preside over this trial. So we made formal request for a different judge, which was granted, and his name was Judge Langdon, and I believe he had been brought in from the Torrington-Wheatland area where he was a district judge.

Now, in Mr. Hanscum's request for the grand jury way back when, and quoted in his letter to Richard Dixon, he had written, "I have reviewed the statutory law in Wyoming, researched some of the case law, and discussed the propriety and purpose of a grand jury with other District Judges." So even though we got another judge, I wondered if they had spoken about this matter before and whether Judge Langdon was coming into this with considerable preconceptions imbedded by Arthur T. Hanscum.

So the first thing we did was get Leazenby and Dooley on the stand and ask them about this report and just see how this accusation against me would stand up to questions under oath. I would like to now bring to light an article that was written by Robert Roten on 9/24/86 which shows how the situation was reported in the newspaper. It told how I had brought a lawsuit against the Sheriff's Department for this kickback report that they had written, and which they hadn't given me so I could defend myself against it, and how it had been maliciously used against me.

The newspaper then described how earlier that day on the stand, Leazenby denied that he had falsified any portion of his report and denied any animosity toward me. He said, instead, that the report was an accurate account of the March 21, 1983 talk with Kevin Dooley. Of course, this incensed me, but that's what he was saying, and I believed he was lying.

But at least the newspaper reported accurately what Dooley had said, because Dooley was called to the stand and had said that he had talked to Leazenby on that date but that Leazenby's report was not true! Further, Dooley specifically denied ever having used the word kickback. In his conversation with Leazenby, he denied telling Leazenby that I had received a penny a gallon kickback for every gallon of gas sold by the gasoline retailers in Laramie as stated in Leazenby's report. One of them had to have been lying.

Now, as this unfolded in front of me, I believed for a certainty right then and there in that courtroom that Leazenby had lied under oath. And I also believed that Dooley had at least told part of the truth when he denied ever accusing me to Leazenby. But I also had to ask myself, why had Dooley ever let Leazenby use this report? He must have had some contact with the sheriff's department while this report was being used to call a grand jury. Now perhaps, his only contact was Leazenby. In which case, he may have not conspired against me with Leazenby, which would have made Leazenby the only rat. But I found out through the next few years that Dooley had kept Leazenby on his payroll as a truck driver, and even though Leazenby may have lied about what he said in his report, I had to wonder about the nature of their relationship. I can only conclude now, after these facts came out in the civil trial, that they may have conspired together to get me indicted for something they both knew all along I never did. I mean, if I had an employee who took the stand under oath and had made statements which indicated I was a liar, knowing they were not true, I'd fire that person.

I might add that one of the first things that I did after I got ahold of that kickback report, was to mail a copy of it to Kevin Dooley at his home, and I sent that by registered mail, and as I expected, I didn't get any comment back from him whatsoever, one way or the other. Now this happened in contrast to his position toward Rex Guice, the man he had named as the one paying me kickbacks in the report. And Dooley had gone to Rex Guice and apologized for the nature of the Leazenby report, and told him that he hadn't meant him any harm by that. So I had to ask myself, why hadn't he extended the same courtesy to me? After all, I was the one that he named as the price fixer and kickback king. And I began to wonder if it wasn't because I was a direct competitor of his in diesel fuel sales. It reminded me of an incident that happened right after we started selling diesel fuel at that location. We were closing at midnight. Sometime between the time we closed, and six AM the next morning, when we reopened, someone had cut all of our diesel hose lines at the pumps. This was about two thousand dollars worth of damage. After that, we stayed open twenty-four hours a day and haven't closed since.

And I recall one conversation we'd had shortly after I opened that diesel station across the street from his Outrider Station. I had dropped the price of diesel fuel about three or four cents per gallon to meet the market selling price of fuel in Cheyenne, Rawlins, and Rock Springs, part of my competition, because the truckers can drive a thousand miles without refueling; so they can pick their spot. To get them to pick me, I had to have a price which matched or beat the price in these other locations on I-80 across Wyoming. And at the time I received a phone call from Kevin Dooley reminding me that diesel fuel wasn't always going to be plentiful, and there might be a shortage as there had been previously, and that to give it away was stupid. As I remember this phone call, I had people in my office at the time that he had called, so I informed him that

I would need to call him back. So I called him back the next day, which is the last time I ever spoke with him, to this day. I told him specifically, "You run your business, and I'll run mine." Now, as I had learned through all this investigation and trials, I can see that what he'd said to me could have been construed as a price fixing attempt. His was a much stronger act than the "survey" which Rex Guice had been called down for. And this made me think that Leazenby had constructed this report in such a way as to leave diesel out of it, so that perhaps neither Dooley or myself would be ask any questions by the grand jury about any possible discussions about diesel prices which we may have had. And I never was asked by the grand jury about diesel or Dooley in that regard, probably because Leazenby had covered the tail of his boss. Now as I went through his deposition and questioning at the grand jury level, none of this was ever mentioned by Dooley either. But Dooley had been asked by the grand jury why I had always marketed at least a penny cheaper on diesel than he had. And he had responded that his station was much newer and he had better facilities in which to draw the customers, including a full-fledged restaurant. So he claimed that he made the decision to let me sell a penny cheaper because of this. Then the grand jury had asked Dooley what would happen if he dropped the price a penny to meet my price, and Dooley had said, and rightly so, that "Foster would just drop the price another penny." So Dooley said he'd just decided to let me sell cheaper.

Now if I had been asked about this by the grand jury, which I hadn't, but if I had I would have told them how I saw it, which was that I had to sell a penny cheaper to actually be at the same price, because he gave away S & H Greenstamps with every purchase, which equals about a penny a gallon in value. Therefore, I sold a penny cheaper, simply to be marketing at the same price, only I gave this value to my customers in cash rather than stamps. Now, I can't help but wonder as I reflect back onto this, why the grand jury didn't recognize me for what I was in Laramie, the low-price setter rather than high-price fixer? And the only conclusion I could rationally make was that the prosecuting attorney and sheriff's department had set out to portray me to all of Laramie as the latter, and the Leazenby report was the only basis they had to try to accomplish this. And all the people of Laramie, or the grand jury for that matter, had to do was to reflect back on what my pricing strategy had been, and it would have been obvious that I had always met prices at the low end of the market, not the high end. There had never been a time that my price was the highest in town.

So I was pleased to see that Dooley had refused to

substantiate the Leazenby report, I was pleased to see that this called Leazenby a liar publicly, and I was not surprised that Leazenby lied under oath. Because this proved to the court conclusively that at least one of them had lied in the report. And I guess I would have to give Mr. Dooley the benefit of the doubt, here. Perhaps he had been used by Leazenby to dupe the town of Laramie, and there was nothing further I could do to prove this, one way or another. At least I now had proof that Dooley denied the words quoted by Leazenby. So Leazenby now, before the eyes of the court, became an exposed rat. This fit together like a glove, and we had shown the court through Dooley and Leazenby that based on testimony under oath, at least one of them was lying for sure, because they contradicted each other. We had proven, without a doubt, that materially the kickback report had no legitimacy. How strong can a case get? I was beginning to feel exonerated in the public eye, and everything I had claimed about my innocence was coming out to be true.

So to win our case, all we had to do was get it into the public record that Dixon had used this report against us.

As we got further into the trial, the main person upon whose testimony our whole case depended on was Richard Dixon. We had not named him in the suit specifically in the hopes that this would leave him available to appear as a witness. But it had come to light with my attorney in different meetings with Judge Langdon that the judge had told my attorney that he was not going to allow Richard Dixon to testify, that he was immune from not only prosecution, but from even having to appear as a witness. When my attorney relayed this information to me, I told him that even if this was going to be the case, I wanted to hear the judge say this with Richard Dixon sitting in the chair in court. I had hoped that once the judge saw that Leazenby had lied in the report and we had proven this in court, that in the spirit of justice, he would then see the importance to me, to society, to Laramie, to all the people, of bringing Leazenby and the sheriff's department into full accountability for their actions. He could have done this without forcing Dixon or the county attorney's office to be accountable also. If he had just decided to allow the subpoena calling Dixon to the stand, we could have had justice.

But we got no justice. When Richard Dixon came into the courtroom and took the stand, Judge John T. Langdon from Torrington said, "Mr. Dixon, I don't want you to say a word unless I tell you to. I don't want you to testify."

So my faith in justice vanished. Because I had just seen an act by Judge Langdon which kept Dixon from testifying, and which saved the face of the other judge, Arthur T. Hanscum, because the judge had used this kickback report to call the grand jury. And as it turned out, there had to be a felony in order to call the grand jury, and the only felony charge they could concoct was the alleged kickback in this report, and the judge had used this as well as Richard Dixon, and the judge had not required that we get the report during our criminal trial. All this was going to come out into public record if Dixon said a word.

So the judge had saved the "system" from having to be ridiculed in public for this farce, and saved the "system" from being held accountable for the results. I couldn't even begin to measure what this had cost me, both in business, in anguish, in my image, to my customers, my whole life.

Well, bearing this cost, and seeing what the judge did, inflamed me in a new and different way. It created a helpless feeling, one of having been raped in public and now watching the rapists go free, protected by one of their own. Everybody knew the facts, the issue was how to get them into the trial record as eveidence. So we had them, but Judge Langdon, in one fell swoop, had sliced our case to ribbons and had not allowed any evidence to emerge by immunizing Richard Dixon from testifying.

It was unbelieveable to me that anybody should be immune

from testimony, prosecution, maybe, but testimony? This was the truth, here, and the public record needed to reflect the truth. This was what our system was all about! I didn't go after these people with guns or clubs or anything unethical, I went after them in the manner prescribed by the laws of the society in which I live, and right here before my eyes, the judge protected the system and thus condoned the use of lies and malicious prosecution and lying sheriff's officers.

My attorney advised me that we had no case without Dixon's testimony, so I did what I had already made the decision to do in advance if we came to this unfortunate crossroads: I dropped the suit the moment that Dixon was gagged, and released silently from the stand. As I looked at him he appeared like he had been gagged with a torn piece of white sheet drawn tightly between his lips and tied behind his head. And I can't say that I saw any dignity here, in his image, or that of the entire proceeding.

So I dropped the suit in total dismay, and the next day the newpaper printed a statement released by Judge Langdon, which said, "It would have been grossly unjust to Sheriff Leazenby for something that maybe the county attorney had done." I could not believe this. How could Judge Langdon possibly feel that Leazenby was not responsible for what he'd written? He'd been accused in Judge Langdon's Court of lying by Dooley. Was he not responsible for his act of lying? Why wasn't this pursued right then and there? Purgery should have been leveled against either him or Dooley, until the rat jumped out of the water. Surely, Judge Langdon had to have known, as I knew by then, that this report had been written intentionally and used intentionally to get what Dixon needed to call a grand jury to get the criminal trials. But knowing this, as he must have, he still felt it would be unjust to Leazenby. Poor, poor Leazenby. Unjust? I loved seeing Judge Langdon use that word, because I knew quite well what unjust meant, I'd seen it all along and now here it was again, being used to cover not only Leazenby but all the people who had used his report.

COMPELLING CIVIC INTEREST

CHAPTER NINE

Now a period of time came here where I had all these feelings and very strong memories about all this, and time, just crept along, and these feelings stayed clear and hard. And the most trying feeling of all was that of the helplessness of it all. The feeling now that there had been absolutely no control over how this happened and what it would do, and then on top of it, no recourse whatsoever. I had spent my efforts to resolve this in court in vain. And now that was spent. Now there was nothing.

It reminded me of what I had learned to have to accept regarding my problem with alcohol: that I was powerless over alcohol and my life had become unmanageable. So I had faced this already in life, and it had been another powerful foe, only this time it was even worse, because this time I had absolutely no control to make a decision to reverse this problem. No matter what I did, it couldn't help. Nobody wanted to listen.

Even in the appearances before the grand jury, and in court, and in the media, nobody wanted to hear my side of it. They weren't going to listen; they didn't hear a word I said even if the sound went to their ears. They were mentally blocked against me. Their determination to convict me at the direction of the deputy county attorney was stoic. He had convinced them I was the rat, and a malicious businessman, a powermonger who abused people and manipulated the whole town. He had convinced them I was so evil that the only way for me to be brought to justice would be through the grand jury. This he had spelled out in that letter to the judge, and with instructions to them, and they all bought it.

Now, in the aftermath, it was the tar baby. Nobody wanted to touch it or address it or listen to me tell how this tar baby had been created and who had created it and how there should be some dirty hands identified. This was a duty which people have in our society, to undo wrongs by society against the innocent. And if the people, the people themselves within what's left of our American way, refuse to act to correct and amend and give retribution to those who have been abused by the power the people give to law enforcement and the courts, then what's left of our American way is diminished by every failure of the people to cause those in power to be responsible for their actions.

In my case, it was perfectly clear who the culprits in "public service" were. I had proof. Irrefutable proof. Not speculation, not intangible conspiracy theories. Proof! And even with this, I had failed to get any response other than to shut the whole thing up and brush it under some old rug in Laramie.

So how could I get this off my mind? I wanted of course for some time to get public awareness on the fact that I had been innocent. Monetary damages were high but less important now than what the people of Laramie would remember of this. I had gone to the newspaper several times to see if they wouldn't do my story, give me some interview and take an editorial stand, or do some feature about this, get this on the front page at least once in an exposé or "day in the life" type story of how I'd been through this and how the community could benefit from this experience, by assuring that safeguards would be followed in the future. But as I spoke with them, I began to realize that they, too, must have made their minds up early. So now it dawned on me that they were not going to change their minds about me, even though I had proven I was innocent, and had proof that the whole business of the grand jury, investigation, charges, and court proceedings had been a deliberate atrocity. I had proof!

The paper wasn't interested. I presented an ad to Ted Duffy, the ad salesman, who took the ad copy to their attorney, Hoke MacMillan, who advised not to print it. So they would not even allow me to buy space to publicize my information about public figures still in office or on the job. There is a need to protect public officials, but how far should this need go?

Now what's important here is that the news media has the power to keep our elected, appointed, and hired officials and police in check of their power. And they can do it. But they have to be willing to do so. They have to believe in truth above self-interest or other interests.

A real journalist could have had a field day. He could have done some award-winning work. He could have literally cleaned up the town of Laramie, and set an example that could have made it very unlikely for this to ever happen there again. The proof that I had been able to obtain to substantiate my worst fears about some of these people was astounding. My worst fears about these people had turned out to be true, and I had proof! Proof that at least the act of lying under oath had been committed, some against me, which resulted in prosecution.

So rather than the newspaper taking the story material, I guess they thought I was being vindictive. They called it sour grapes. Anything I had to say. So it was all on me now, as if I had brought this all on myself. And in this light, it simply took the wind out of my sails. I had no inner tranquility, and literally approached the state of mind of a madman.

So I watched them do nothing and my feeling of helplessness, and some fear of course, fed an anger which continued to build without my control. I was out of control. I was becoming a different person. I didn't feel the same inside, and I didn't like it. I had never been an angry man in my life. And never thought I would become one. And now I had the struggle of trying to keep my anger from turning to hate.

But as this happened, another realization occured to me which enabled me to focus my life again, to try to get some control. It was the realization that the basis of my fear for these people was over. They had spent themselves trying to ruin me. And they spent big trying to do this. And they had thrown all their shots at me, and they all turned out to be blanks. So they scared me, all right, anybody gets scared when they're shot at.

But now that it was over, I was no longer under their

complete control. Now this is different from the alcohol problem, because if I'd let it, alcohol would control and destroy my life in a heartbeat, today, this very day, every day of the rest of my life. But these people were through controlling me. It was no longer the case where I had to just sit and be quiet and take it and wait for a fate which they seemed able to perpetrate on me, or watch myself be destroyed, wondering what they would do next. So the external battle with them was over, but not the internal battle. The internal battle went on. And it was twofold: One, how would I get my normal feeling back inside of myself, and two, how would I deal with my feelings about the system and society?

We all owe something to society. And if we feel strongly about something, we have a duty to act. If we don't, then I think we deserve whatever we get. This gets hard to swallow when you get what I got.

So I felt a duty here to do something. I tried with the newspaper, and I spoke out to everyone I saw. Even if it was simply displaced aggression, I did it. I had some remark every time I saw a sheriff's officer. Even knowing it was the leadership which was the problem, and not all the officers themselves. I still couldn't help the remarks because it was all I had. It had to come out somewhere.

But the only true solice came to me in just a sliver of a tiny thought. It was just a tiny, tiny idea, and as I thought about it I realized it was the only thing I could do which might help me. And that was the idea that I write a book and tell my story for those who would read it.

So even though a few bad people had taken advantage of the power vested in them by the people, and others in power had let them go in spite of their deeds, at least there was this one last avenue which we hold dear in America: and that's freedom of speech. The freedom to write and tell the story of events such as those I'd been through. And there is the right to criticize public officials when they do wrong.

So the newspaper wouldn't do it. I decided I would.

Now this has been some undertaking, because I haven't done any writing in my life. And realized I hadn't done much reading. I had been a hard worker, and if main-street practicality and hard work will get you to heaven, I'm on my way. But reading, I just hadn't done it. So I guess this is a positive for me out of this experience, because it brought me to a new form of expression. Because of my business experiences and practical approach to life, I looked at my age and capabilities, and knew I was going to have to have help. Just like with drinking. I had a major undertaking here, a complex story to tell, and I had a great deal to learn about how it could work.

143

So I made the decision and dedicated myself. And I hoped, as I did this, that the process of writing this story and trying to get it published would get these feelings of mine into some final resolution. There was a very strong hope in me that a book would do this. It would at the very least, serve as a memoir for me and my family and the town of Laramie, a memoir of my side of the story, and a testimony of how much damage a malicious prosecution can do to a man and his family, and how little can be done about it if those people don't have the prior knowledge to know how to protect themselves if something like this gets started.

So I hoped that by writing this story, I could preserve the special information which the public needs to know about regarding grand juries, how they get requested and appointed, what their function is supposed to be in society, and how the people can protect themselves against abuse. Because in the aftermath of all this, I now had this special knowledge. I had learned a lot by this. And if it ever happened to me again, it would be very different. I know enough now to protect myself. But I must also say, that I could only protect myself somewhat. Because a grand jury is an awesome force, and if it is merely the tool of a malicious or unethical prosecutor linked with a malleable or sleeping judge, the grand jurors can be manipulated and the destructive force can be incredible. So part of this story, too, must be to share this information about what constitutes a proper formation of a grand jury, and hopefully people can learn how to be better grand jurors. Because a smart grand juror can think for himself, and if the grand jurors know enough, they could detect an illegal call for their service, by demanding for example, to see the incriminating evidence presented by the prosecutor to the judge, and examining it, and making sure that there is an actual need for the grand jury. If they had done this in my case, they would have seen that a felony was required to justify their calling, and that in my case, this supposed felony was based on hearsay and created by the deputy himself in the kickback report. The real purpose of the grand jury had been the issue of price fixing, which was only a misdemeanor, and not sufficient cause to call a grand jury. Any attorney general, like the one in Wyoming, could tell the public this.

But I knew that the public would never get this information, or any benefit of my experience unless I wrote it myself.

Now with this last sense of duty, to make this information available to the public, I began to feel my anger at the system come under control. I now could not only get this out and tell my side of the story, I could feel that I had done my duty to society to try to correct the wrong, not only for my benefit, because that time had passed, but for the benefit of society. I would know I had done my best in what I felt as a strong sense of duty. Because if I just let this go, then I'm part of the problem which I think is destroying America. And that is, the people are losing their rights, and getting walked on by power abusers, and taking their abuse and doing nothing about it.

Now what's really sad is that when I tried to do something about this in the court system, the court system rendered themselves immune from even having to tell the truth under oath in public. So they shut the truth out of the courtroom. And they shut the truth out of society. Or so they thought. Because they may have the power to protect themselves by shutting the truth out of their little courtrooms in Laramie, but they don't have the power to shut the truth out of a book.

So I set out to write the book about this. This is not to be a book of fiction, this is based on fact and truth. I decided to let it all out, and let the public see these people, and even myself, and let the public read this if they will, and the public can decide what's important here, what's right and wrong, and what justice is, or isn't. And the public can decide about the future, and hopefully this book will help contribute to a better future.

Now this may all sound high and mighty, but I realized I had to do it, even if it meant the unpleasant and even self-

146

serving task of exposing what I consider to be bad people and bad things they've done, because these people were and are in positions of public power and public office, and they should be held accountable for their acts just like the common people. They enforce those same laws against all the people. We hire them to do this, and they have a duty to enforce those laws against their own, if need be, to keep their own ranks honest. They have a duty to live a higher standard because of their public positions and the trust that we, the people, put in them, the kind of trust that made my mother believe that just because they came after me, I must have done something. So high and mighty or not, my only recourse was to write the book and at least hold them accountable in my own eyes and any eyes who would read the book. And let them read it too. Because this is the forum, and the only forum, which I have left as an American, and I suppose anybody can challenge anything if they want. But I decided I'd fulfill my duty here, to myself, my family, and society, and would not run from this challenge.

As I got into this issue of duty to society, the feeling got stronger in me, because I saw crime everywhere in society, and Laramie too, which I will describe, and seeing all this crime, it seemed absurd that some people use the grand jury to create crime for their ends. And I speak here about the way Jeff was set up by someone's sending the milkman to entrap him. And a lot of public money was spent, but when I let other authorites know about some of the injustices I discovered while putting my story together to write, the other authorities were just like the newspaper. They didn't care, and they wouldn't prosecute even with prima facie evidence. Now what kind of society has Laramie become?

I sincerely hope that this trend in Laramie can be reversed, and that the authorities will begin prosecuting all crimes, especially when the criminals are public officials. Only then will Laramie be a safe place to live. Only then will it be a functioning, law-based society, when crime is prosecuted, not precipitated by the system.

CHAPTER TEN

Several aspects pertaining to the people and the actions of the attempted prosecution against me led me in the nature of my inquiries. The outcome of my discoveries is quite a surprise. I wanted to know what kind of people, if there are kinds of people, would carry out such an endeavor, and why, and what would be their motivations.

Since I had been scrutinized in a most unpleasant way, I felt that those who falsely accused me and went through my record of life with a fine tooth comb deserved the same. More so, actually, because it was they, and not I, who served in public jobs. So I looked for information which would help me to understand these people, perhaps enable me to forgive them, or at least know enough about them to decide whether they deserved forgiveness.

I think this was a rational approach, but a very negative feeling was to be thrown at me like mud, as another accusation against me, that I was only interested in "getting back at them." Now I'll address this here. The newspaper editors had apparently felt that way, and some others in the community, like Barry Johnson, said things which indicated this approach to the matter. This is a man that I have known most of my life, at least I thought I knew him. I was having coffee in a coffee shop with a friend of mine by the name of Gail, and I had mentioned the need for honesty in our law enforcement people. And without warning, Barry Johnson began to verbally abuse me. I don't remember ever being talked to by anyone in a more offensive manner than the way Barry talked to me. I was stunned to the point that I refused to even respond to him at that particular moment. He had told me that he didn't want to listen to my feelings toward the law enforcement people, and I wanted to remind him that I hadn't been speaking to him, he'd been eavesdropping, but there was no room for a word edgewise as he continued to castigate me, loudly and in public. It was so rude and I was so shocked that I just got out of my seat and left the restaurant without saying even a single word to him. This had bothered me for quite some time. I mean, I thought Barry was a friend of mine, and I felt the need to contact Barry Johnson and ask him the question, why had he done this, and for what purpose? So I waited until one day when I saw his truck at a different restaurant, and Gail's truck was also there. So I went in with the specific purpose of asking Barry, and said to him, "Barry, you may not know how badly you hurt my feelings or how stunned I was at the manner in which you spoke to me, now I have to ask you, why did you do this, and for what purpose?"

His response had been that he simply didn't want to talk with me then and there, but would speak with me about it later. So I asked him to please give me a call, and I would be more than happy to meet with him at his convenience to discuss this. After a certain amount of time passed without my receipt of a phone call from Barry, I then approached him again in the same place that I had asked him the first time, and it seems that most of the same people were in there. He informed me that he was going out of town for a few days and he would get ahold of me when he got back. And as of this writing, I have not yet heard from him.

It's not my intent to ever contact Barry Johnson again about this subject, but I think this incident illustrates what the general sentiment of the town became toward me after the false prosecution. I can only interpret his words and his defense of the sheriff's department as conveying his belief that they had done right to come after me, that they should have gotten me, and that even if they had been dishonest in their attempt to convict me, this was less important than the general issue of getting gasoline prices lowered in Laramie. Thus, the need for cheap gas became more important than law enforcement principles or justice. So for me to say in public that the deputies had done wrong would offend someone who had this general sentiment. To remind them that it had been an illegal attempt would arouse anger, and rather than face that issue, it was easier for people like Barry Johnson to mistake my criticism of the sheriff's department for sour grapes than to understand the true importance and meaning of my words to the community. At least Barry said what he did to my face, rather than behind my back. But his refusal to talk with me later showed that he, like others, didn't want to face the deep issues which the grand jury action had raised about the integrity of the law in Laramie. It was easier to think that I was simply vindictive. I had to ask myself, what would Barry's words to me have been if he had been through a similar smear and prosecution, or if it had been his family they had come after with false reports? There isn't much I can do but shrug.

The deepest understanding as to why this event and other similar events had happened came down to the fact that some people in Laramie felt that gasoline prices in town were artificially high. And even though I was always competing with the lowest price in Laramie, not the high end but the low end of prices, just because I was visible in the community, I had been the easiest to target. I had shown success, and success in the gas business had been interpreted as illegal price tactics. Now this was just a feeling around town, but a strong one, and this feeling, coupled with an ambitious deputy county attorney trying to make a name for himself and trying to cement his future in Laramie, had resulted in the judge and prosecuting attorney placing gasoline prices as a public interest which superseded the discovery of or necessity of a crime, in order to call a grand jury and launch an investigation.

Now these people who came after me used "public interest" as their reason for "good intentions." So when I asked myself, did they really care about public interest? As I looked into their past, I was quite surprised, because the things I found showed me that they were looking out for themsleves, not the public. And seeing the proof of this led me to the conclusion that they had been grand standing in the political arena and the press, not really caring about the fact that they had no evidence.

So I decided first of all to find out what the costs in terms of dollars had been for the county to call and assemble the grand jury, and carry it out. So I went to Frank Moore, Albany County Commissioner, with whom I'd spent four years on the City Council. I felt that this man knew me well. He knew my principles, and had to know how I thought because we had discussed many major issues for the City of Laramie in all those public discussions on the city council. I also knew that the county commissioners had to give their blessing before a grand jury could be called, because they basically had to approve the money that it was going to cost the people, before the money could be spent. I already knew that the deputy county attorney, Richard Dixon, had previously been involved with a grand jury called in the Wheatland area of Wyoming, and had stated that this grand jury had cost three quarters of a million dollars, and had produced negative results.

So I felt our county commissioners should have already had some feel for what it would cost to call a grand jury in Albany County, and I wanted the people to know what this fiasco had cost them in public money. And the figure is unbelievable. I had asked Commissioner Moore for his help to let us know how much this cost, because Karen Maurer, County Attorney, had refused our request to reveal publicly this cost. The answer from Commissioner Moore astonished me. He said, "Dick, I can't do anything really about this, I'm only an elected official." So he refused authority to release the information. But he should have remembered that it took his authority, along with two other commissioners, Frank Lilly, and Max Rardin, to approve this action in the first place because of the added cost which would come out of their budget.

I kept pressing, through an attorney and through perseverance. I circulated a petition requesting this cost of the grand jury be disclosed by Karen Maurer to the public, and over ninety people signed it. We continued to ask Karen Maurer and others in a public manner. She knew that others were being pressed also, and it got to a point that she finally felt she had to give an answer to the public. So on January 12, 1984, an article in the *Laramie Daily Boomerang* addressed the question of cost and Karen Maurer got the monkey off her back. The figure that she gave to the newspaper was $6,185.36. This was astounding! Richard Dixon had previously set the figure for the Wheatland area grand jury at three quarters of a million dollars, and she sets this number? Who is kidding who? I simply say to County Attorney Maurer, that I wish I could hire my attorneys, and all those sheriff's officers, and all the court expenses, for the length of time of the investigation, the whole investigation and criminal trials took about a year, and I simply say further that it is unbelieveable that they would belittle themselves by telling this to the people of Laramie. Do the people of Laramie actually believe that seventeen indictments into the gas industry had been brought together for $6,185.36? I think by saying so, she had presented the deal of the century to the people. Boy howdy, had they gotten a deal. Seventeen indictments, none of which held up in court, with one exception: the milkman's testimony which accused my son of blackmail. So now, the fiasco against me had become the deal of century for the legal arm of the county.

Well I can show how the county spent similar sums of money with a lot less fanfare. In fact, with no fanfare at all. Perhaps they don't want the public to know the real numbers about anything in Laramie. Well, I couldn't ever get the real number on the cost of the grand jury, except by comparison, which sets it as a healthy portion of a million dollars.

So in terms of various costs, let's take our first look at the milkman, who claimed his livelihood had been destroyed by me and my family, who claimed he lost his sanity, had to see the preacher. He sold his business to another milk company, which didn't surprise me because he had even offered it to me, and milkman Dubard, just five days after the trial, with his bad back, weak mind, and sanity questions, was hired as a sheriff's officer by Don Fritzen, the County Sheriff. For them to hire their only witness, just five days after a trial in which the poor man stated he was unfit to be a milkman anymore, certainly shocked me. Whether it's legal or not, it does not seem fitting in any sense of ethics for a sheriff to hire a witness so quickly after the trial, especially when his claim of mental unfitness was a necessary element to create the charge of blackmail. But now if you look at this, and remember that the milkman had come to my son out of the blue, it sure looks like solicitation of a crime, and it looks to me like it could have been planned all long. Perhaps the milkman had been promised a job if he would just set my family up for blackmail. Now I must mention that some six months before all of this, the milkman had come to me, to me mind you, because he knew it would be me he would have to ask and not my son, but he came to me and ask me to buy him out of his business. He told me he wasn't making it, and wanted to get out of the business. I didn't buy it because we had no desire to get into the milk business. But how convenient for the milkman to later claim in trial testimony that because of us he was no longer fit to run this business. Convenient for him. Convenient for the sheriff's department, the judge, the prosecuting attorney, very convenient. Brilliant, for anyone who may have helped him come to Jeff with just the right sentence to present.

So miraculously, the milkman had been saved from his economic plight, unfit for his old line of work, but determined to be quite fit by the sheriff in just five days. So what, may we ask, is this cost to the county, for these wages? In my mind, I add them to the cost of the grand jury.

Now one of the reasons I add this on, is because of other expenditures which the sheriff's office paid which suit some very special interests, such as the personal interest of the sheriff himself. Every month the county pays their bills by voucher, and the monthly record gets published in the newspaper. As Fate would have it, my brother Bob is a master electrician and also a journeyman plumber, and had read a voucher which had been paid to Donald Fritzen, described as for jail plumbing, in the amount of $965.55, and another voucher paid to Edna Lee Robinson, a female sheriff, for $694.35, also for jail plumbing. On this same month of vouchers, there was one more voucher paid to James B. Ide (the deputy who had fingerprinted us and laughed while he was doing it), for tree trimming in the amount of $210.00. This trimming, when I looked at the receipt, was for bushes and trees on the Albany County Courthouse premises. My first thought, knowing that Mr. Ide wasn't a tree trimmer by trade, was to wonder what equipment he had used to accomplish this trimming. But equipment aside, the Jack of All Trades seemed to apply to those in the sheriff's department. Now when I think about the fact that some of my family are involved in the trades, such as plumbing, and I think about how licensing is required, and certain other business requirements before any of my family can bid on public jobs, I wonder how this work got bid, and why it was allowed to be performed without licenses?

Does being a sheriff license you to be a plumber? And further, when you head the office which authorizes the work, is there a responsibility to the public for how their money gets spent? Well I think so. And when I compare this lack of responsibility and ethics to that which I saw during the investigation, and after, with hiring a witness, and the interlocking of the flow of money between sheriff's deputies and county purse strings, between sheriff's deputies and others who turned out to be my competitors in the gasoline business, all this money and how it flowed began to shape my opinion about how the grand jury had been formed and how the general ethics of public service did not apply in Laramie.

So upon a couple of visits to the courthouse by myself and my brother, the journeyman plumber, we discovered the receipts, and checked through the proper records to see if Sheriff

Fritzen was a licensed plumber. We knew that in order to provide plumbing service to a commercial building, it was illegal to provide such services without the participation of a licensed, master plumber. I had thought the City of Laramie would have shown an interest in this, because of the many times we have not been allowed to do work for them, even though we were in the contracting business, because they had always been adament about requiring a master plumber for any plumbing work, even though my brother was a journeyman. So we had been told we didn't have the right to do any of the work ourselves.

It turned out, not to our surprise, that neither Sheriff Donald Fritzen and nor Deputy Edna Robinson was licensed to do plumbing in Laramie. So we went to the courthouse and requested the receipts for these vouchers to see what, specifically, jail house plumbing they had performed for the county. And much to our surprise and amazement, as we pored through the receipts turned into the county commissioners for payment, there wasn't so much as a receipt for a leaky faucet which had been turned in for payment. Money had been paid, but not for plumbing! Surprise, surprise. Some of the items we found and I have record of, were on Mr. Fritzen's credit card. One, in particular, was a credit card charge for $433.56 spent by

Mr. Fritzen at Corral West, a local western clothing store, which showed no description of merchandise whatever, just "miscellaneous items." Now this was one of the receipts turned in for jail plumbing. We felt we had to look into this, so we called the store and asked if they by some freak chance sold any products related to plumbing. You can image the laughter with the response, "No! We're in the clothing business." Whatever was spent there, it couldn't have been for plumbing.

The receipts for the remainder of the $965.55 expenses were also credit card purchases by him throughout the county, and none of these were for plumbing, either.

Now when we checked out Edna Robinson's receipts, in the amount of $694.35, we found that none of her receipts were for jail plumbing either. The main receipt for $375.00 amazed me the most: it was an adding machine tape, torn off a machine, signed by Sheriff Fritzen, for car washing, which I assume he means she must have washed cars for the department. It doesn't take a genius to figure out that at even five dollars a car, you would have to wash seventy five cars to earn this money. Now I have never seen a sheriff's patrol car washed anywhere near the courthouse, or at any private residence. So I had to wonder at this. Washing cars and calling it plumbing?

Now after I discovered this in public records, the proof was very solid, and I felt like doing something about it. I felt I had discovered prima facie evidence of corruption, and diversion of public money to private pockets. After due consideration, I felt that I had to bring to light to the community how their public dollars were being appropriated. Now I add here that if in the investigation of seven years of my records by the FBI, they had found anything even remotely as fishy as this, I would have been indicted and fully prosecuted and convicted, and rightly so. I guess this made me feel that some of those who had falsely accused me, deserved to have some authorities review their records, and conceivably prosecute them based on the evidence uncovered. How could the county leadership let this money slide into the pockets of sheriff's department personnel so deceivingly? I simply point out that this is not lawful, and the public shouldn't stand for it. It amounts to giving public money to law enforcement officers under false pretenses, perhaps even giving jobs under false pretenses, the milkman?

My brother and I discussed the issue of what we should do about this. It was our personal feeling that we should do something. So we came up with what we called the factmobile. And we put the numbers of the vouchers on large signs on the truck and parked it in front of the courthouse, feeling that there should be enough public interest in this that somebody would want to know why these funds had been diverted to the sheriff's department for jail plumbing. This apparently wasn't the case, because as far as we know, nobody ever even questioned this, including radio, including the newspaper, who you would think would take any opportunity to clean up any underhandedness or corruption. Nothing ever happened. The only thing we ever saw was the hate coming out of Sheriff Fritzen's eyes as he went to work in the mornings and looked at the green factmobile parked in front of his courthouse.

I must mention here, what I had felt when forced by my own ethics to resign as director of The Citizens Bank of Laramie just because I had been indicted, just because I was publicly accused of a crime, even though it turned out there was no proof even to begin with. I had lost my good public image because of people like Sheriff Fritzen who were supposed to be doing their job, not plumbing, not lining the pockets of deputics, or allowing false kickback reports to be written and used to form a grand jury.

Now Leazenby turned out to be a fine one. Guess who he worked for, all along while he wrote this kickback report? The very gasoline dealer who was my competitor, the very dealer Leazenby declared innocent of any price fixing (on the basis of diesel sales!). So it reads like a fairy tale when it comes out in its entirety. Leazenby says he'll "get what's needed" to get me, and claims in a report that his boss, whom he protects in the same report, has accused me of forcing kickbacks from other dealers, and naming Rex Guice as one of those paying me kickbacks. So Leazenby, this gasoline truck driver who calls himself a sheriff's deputy, points the finger at two of his boss's competitors. His oath of office is to protect the people of the county from crime.

So I now had to carry the smear of the false charges, and discovering that the sheriff who wrote the false report worked for one of my competitors caused quite a sting to my feelings. The weave of all these corrupt acts among sheriff's officers, and their connections and jobs in the gasoline industry, raised a very serious question about whether this had been an inside job to use the office to run me out of business.

Well, they had ruined my reputation, false as their shots at me had been. They did destroy my reputation. I would feel the repercussions from this for the rest of my life. Some people in Laramie would never forget, and would never look at how the outcome had showed me innocent. They would never look at that. Just like nobody seemed to want to look at the corruption in the sheriff's department.

So this is their security. Or is it? Is the public secure, when these things go on unpunished? Or is only the office of the sheriff secure, because they got away with it then, and therefore can continue to get away with it if steps are not taken to force accountability. And only the people can do this. I'll guarantee that if Judge John Langdon would have allowed the trial against the sheriff's office to continue, all this would have come out, and Laramie could have taken a good look at their law enforcement as it was really working.

Denied that, I just give a little glimpse here to show what would have come out. Perhaps this is just the tip of the iceburg, but if you're a ship at sea and come into the port of Laramie, be careful of this iceberg lest it sink your ship if you touch it.

Now I went ahead and notified the proper authorities of the false plumbing payments to the sheriff's officers when I saw that the factmobile was not accomplishing any legal action. Now these payments, made public in the newspaper, had receipts which bore the signatures of the three county commissioners approving the payment of these vouchers. The three commissioners were Frank Lilly, Frank Moore, and Leah Talbott. Now I had to ask myself, and this was uncomfortable, because I don't have anything against these people, but had I done something similar in the gasoline business it may have been labeled a crime. Now I suppose that even if the commissioners got called down for this in an investigation, it may simply be called malfeasance of office at most. But in my eyes it was worse.

Now these are the people who approved the cost of the grand jury. This, they apparently didn't want made public any more than the cost and details of jailhouse plumbing.

None of the authorities I presented this prima facie evidence to would take action. Again, the people in the system were protecting other people in the system. So I decided to take one more final step. I made contact with Stan Hunt, State Bank Examiner, the man who had been somewhat involved in the matter of my resignation from the bank board, and I told him what I had and how I felt about this jail plumbing, and he suggested I write to Governor Herschler, and that the governor would have the authority to require an audit. So I took his advice and on August 19, 1986 I did write a letter to the governor, by registered mail. This is what it said:

Dear Governor,

Enclosed is a copy of the *Laramie Boomerang* showing county expenditures and payments for the month of June 1986. As you can see Donald L. Fritzen was paid $965.55 for jail plumbing. Fritzen is our sheriff. He is not a licensed plumber. Also a payment of $694.35 was made to Edna Mae Robinson for jail plumbing. She is the deputy sheriff and again not a licensed plumber. J. .B. Ide was also paid

$210.00 for courthouse repairs. He is also a deputy sheriff. I checked into it thoroughly and found the above and none of it was for plumbing. In fact, most invoices are adding machine tapes and are not even clear to what they are. To show these payments to the public as plumbing in my opinion is fraud. And as a concerned citizen I believe it should be checked out. I mailed a copy of the enclosed to our Wyoming State Auditor a few days ago. Yesterday I received a call from Stan Hunt. He suggested I inform you and with your permission he would audit this. I would also suggest that the evidence locker at the sheriff's office should be audited. Thank you for your kind consideration for the above.

Respectfully yours,
Dick Foster

Now note the second to last sentence, where I suggested in addition to an audit of finances, an audit of the evidence locker at the sheriff's department might be in order. I felt that if the sheriff was receiving public money under the pretense of plumbing, the easiest other place to get property would have been from the evidence locker.

I sent a copy of this letter to Stan Hunt as a courtesy, to show that I had followed his advice.

As it turned out, all this was just the tip of the iceburg, because I received information that a former deputy sheriff who had worked under Fritzen made it known to the Wyoming Department of Criminal Investigation (DCI) that there was a possibility that cocaine had been stolen from the evidence locker and used by members of the department. So I wondered if my letter had any bearing on the initiation of the investigation, and I felt that it hadn't. I believe my letter had been interpreted by those people as sour grapes, and they too would have protected those in the system. In fact, one of their investigators came to see me and although no mention of the letter to the governor was made, I was asked by this gentleman why I had suggested that maybe the evidence locker at the sheriff's department be audited. This led me to believe that he must have had some knowledge of the letter to the governor. I had answered his question by simply saying, "If you have a department such as this sheriff's department which is involved in false payments for plumbing, and writing false kickback reports about people, common sense would tell you that there's probably a lot more going on there. And the locker is controlled solely by the sheriff."

And it turned out that my hunch was right. Although my recommendation to audit had apparently been taken as sour grapes, the suggestion by a former deputy had been taken seriously. There was an investigation, and the results became public, that there had been cocaine theft out of the evidence locker and it came to light that the thefts were by other deputy sheriffs: one, who was Donald Fritzen's son, and another female officer. Due to their investigation they found that Deputy Fritzen had stolen cocaine out of the evidence locker and had used the cocaine himself. Now Sheriff Don Fritzen, before this investigation revealed these thefts of cocaine from the evidence locker, must have anticipated that this would at some point become public. So Sheriff Fritzen, in advance, took it upon himself to send his son, one of the deputies accused of the theft, to Fort Collins, Colorado for a drug rehabilitation program, a program put out by another arm of the law enforcement system themselves, to get his son rehabilitated so that when his son got caught, he could say he had already handled the situation. So he himself had already made the decision as to what the punishment for his son should be for this theft and useage of cocaine. He had also said that the cocaine had not been used by his son while on duty as a sheriff's officer. So his son was never prosecuted for this, and this would have never come to light had it not been for another sheriff's deputy who had finally decided that enough was enough in this sheriff's department. I might add that the rehabilitation costs had been presented to the Albany County Commissioners, and were approved for payment and paid by the county.

Now I must add that Sheriff Fritzen, in addition to getting

the milkman on the payroll as a deputy, had two sons and a brother-in-law also on the payroll as deputies. During his tenure, the department had grown from approximately ten or fifteen officers, to over forty! If you look in the newspaper, you'll see that the department gets about two phone calls a day for law enforcement assistance: half of these are about as serious as that of a barking dog. And the highest percentage of serious complaints is of drunken drivers. It's a very crime-free county when compared to practically anywhere in the US.

Now when Donald Fritzen sent his son down for rehabilitation, he later told the press that his son didn't get paid while he was down there, his son had been removed from the payroll. This was not true. His son not only got paid, he got paid overtime during that month. Now the next sheriff to be elected after Fritzen was Glenn Bennett, the other officer who had been involved with the making of the Leazenby report. And Bennett was the sheriff when the issue of Fritzen's son made the newspapers, and he had been asked also about whether Fritzen's son had received pay while under rehabilitation, and Bennett had also stated that Fritzen's son was not paid during the rehabilitation. The news writer did what I had done to check it out, and found what I had: that Fritzen's son got paid, and even got paid overtime during that month. This time the newspaper did its job. The writer confronted Bennett with his discoveries, and Bennett shrugged it off with, "Oh? Well, I thought he didn't get paid."

Now I had to go to the courthouse to find these records, but I did it because the audacity of the sheriff never ceased to amaze me. Now the end of the term of office was near for Fritzen, and he declared that he was not going to seek another term as sheriff. Now I heard that he was supporting another officer in the department to run for the job, but just before the election, he suddenly switched his support away from this officer and toward another one, a man by the name of Glenn Bennett. Remember this name? This was the lead investigator for price fixing in Laramie, the man who stood in the corner at Dooley's Truck Stop, conveniently out of earshot, while Leazenby "interrogated" Kevin Dooley, his boss. It is my belief that after he backwashed on support for this other deputy who was running for the office, he had created some bad blood in the department.

Now I'll point out that when I was drinking I had been drinking for years before I was ever referred to or felt the need for rehabilitation. Now, would a sheriff's deputy who used cocaine feel the need for rehabilitation after just "one useage?" I guess I have to say, that again the people in the system protected themselves, and in this, it even went within a family. It seems incredible that it would be a deputy's own father who would make the decision to prosecute or not prosecute for theft of cocaine from the evidence locker.

Yet today, it is Deputy Fanning, Fritzen's brother-in-law, who holds the number two position in the Albany County Sheriff's Office. And it is he who made the remark recently that he felt that Fritzen had handled all this about his son correctly. But this makes sense to me only when I acknowledge the fact that Fanning is a brother-in-law to Donald Fritzen. His opinion is absurd when all the facts are known, and it shows me that the problems which I discovered about Fritzen's tenure as sheriff, probably still continue with Fanning and others in the department, because Fanning is covering up the real history of the department with statements like the one he made.

It's just like Nixon and Halderman. Now I must point out that it was as absurd to expect Fritzen to prosecute his own son for cocaine theft as it would have been to expect me to prosecute my own son for the blackmail charges they concocted. So facing this, it irks me that his son got off and never got charged. And Leazenby is still there too, in the sheriff's department.

There was one thing that was done by the present county

attorney. He had told Fritzen that his son would have to resign from the sheriff's department, or he would be prosecuted. But I must ask why the county attorney took it upon himself to let the deputy, who was sworn under oath to enforce the law and then broke it himself, a felony theft, resign and go free. What a deal. How would this sit with a cocaine offender doing five or ten or twenty years in prison for a similar offense?

Now it had come out that being a sheriff was a stressful job, and that the theft and use of cocaine had been caused by stress. Now if somebody wants to know what stress is, just ask me what I felt when my family and I were publicly accused of blackmail. That, my friends, will create stress, some real stress.

So I will hope that as I finish this book that some of the stress which lingers in me will dissipate. Perhaps it will only dissipate if and when I ever see the people in Laramie, or perhaps anywhere in America, stand up to this abuse of public offices, and tolerate it no further. My question to the people of Laramie is, are we going to tolerate dope theft by the very people who get it by arresting other people for having it? I hope not. And the only hope I see is for the people to express their outrage at such events, to express their desire to prosecute such wrongdoings within law enforcement. And to expect those in law enforcement to live by the same rules we do, and be held accountable when they don't.

COMPELLING CIVIC INTEREST

CHAPTER ELEVEN

It is the entirety of the way in which the sheriff's deputies of Albany County have conducted themselves which raises the biggest challenge for the people of Laramie. When I say entirety of conduct, I mean the audacity and broad scope of activity which is blatantly illegal. Now some of these offenses are big ones, such as false vouchers and false reports to incriminate and indict citizens. But it is the sum of the big offenses and the little ones which reveal the whole picture, the root of the problem in terms of our modern life in America. And I go on to say

175

America here, because of statements by policemen like Mark Fuhrman to the effect that these men think they are gods, and can do anything they want, that their power is absolute, and they will never be held accountable for their abuses. When people take this view of their position in law enforcement, then even a small city like Laramie can see the outcome, if the people will only choose to take a good look.

The petty offenses which Leazenby, by way of example, has committed, perhaps for the benefit of either Kevin Dooley, himself, or both of them, by driving a fuel truck overloaded beyond legal limits to save freight and tax money, illustrate how a law enforcement officer's arrogance can lead him to break the law when he wants and have the confidence that he will never be charged or prosecuted or fined or imprisoned or held accountable in any way. The sad logic of this is, those citizens who also want to break the law can hire sheriff's deputies to carry out their needs, and they also know that they are protected by the veil of the deputy's badge.

This is how it works. Leazenby worked part time for Dooley as a truck driver. He would go with an empty fuel truck from Laramie to Sinclair or Cheyenne or whatever refinery or terminal had the fuel he was to pick up. It just so happened that on November 21, 1985, Leazenby was loading one of Dooley's trucks at Sinclair Refinery at the same time one of my drivers was loading our truck at the same refinery. My drivers are specifically told before they go, exactly what product and quantity they are to load and pull back to the station. The major reason for this is to ensure that they are pulling a legal load on the highway. We must watch this fairly closely, because gasoline and diesel have different weights, deisel weighing approximately one pound more per gallon than gas. So the legal quantity is based in part on what the product is.

We have a truck with a capacity of 9,500 gallons of either gas or diesel. If we load a full legal limit of gasoline only, we can pull 8,400 gallons per load. If we are pulling diesel, we can only legally load about 7,500 gallons to haul. If we have both fuels loaded (in separate compartments on the same truck), then we have to calculate weight and load accordingly. We do this at our main office in Laramie, and when we give a driver a load to pull from the refinery, he is told what he will load. The main reason for this is to see that he is actually pulling legal limits on the highway, we don't leave it up to him. We do this to be responsible, and feel that all companies should instruct their drivers to load legal.

But on this date of November 21, 1985, John Leazenby was filling up the tanker he was driving for Dooley Oil at the same time my driver was loading a truck for us. Two years had passed since the grand jury investigated me, and Leazenby had called Dooley a liar in the civil trial, and it surprised my driver that Leazenby would still be working for Dooley.

So as they were loading, my driver recognized that Leazenby had just loaded a full 9,500 gallons of diesel. This is 2,000 gallons over the legal limit. Dooley's truck was indentical to the one which we own, and his legal limits were the same as our legal limits. So when our driver came back to Laramie he told me about this, and was wondering why a person such as John Leazenby was being allowed to pull illegal loads when I wouldn't allow the same thing in my company, which would have saved us money.

With an extra 2,000 gallons on each load, four loads would eliminated the need for the fifth trip. That's quite a savings, ton per mile road taxes, drivers wages, and cost of running the truck for the fifth load. I told him we were gonna haul legal. That wasn't the way I wanted to save money. I didn't know whether it was Dooley Oil Company's decision, or the decision of drivers like Leazenby as to what load they would pull on the highway, but the fact that Leazenby was a deputy sheriff made me wonder if he would ever be stopped and checked for his load, and if so, would another officer give him the same ticket that my driver would get? And further, did the fact that he was a deputy mean that he had a higher standard to live up to on the highway?

I asked myself, how would it look if there were an accident caused by the excessive weight, and the public found out a deputy had loaded it and driven it?

So I decided to find out what the reaction would be, without waiting for an accident or other precipitous act. I asked my driver, on his next trip to Sinclair, to go into the office and ask if they would give him copies of the load ticket for the one he saw loaded by Leazenby. The individual on duty thought about it for a moment, and then agreed, saying that he didn't see anything wrong with that, and gave my driver also, the copies of tickets for what had been pulled out of the refinery for the past two days.

We found that Leazenby had pulled four loads from Sinclair to Laramie in that two day period. Two of the loads were full capacity of 9,500 gallons, overloaded by 2,200 gallons, or approximately 15,400 pounds overweight per load. The other two were also overloaded, but not the full maximum. By my calculations of costs, these four overloads saved Dooley Oil Company $180.03.

Now I had to ask myself, why would Leazenby be willing

to put himself in a position to pull these overloads? I felt it was a direct affront to his duty as a deputy. And I also felt that the protection of Leazenby's badge against possible tickets on the highway for this was an unfair competitive advantage for Dooley Oil Company. When I imagined how often this happened and how much money it would amount to over a long period of time, I recognized that the situation created an unfair business market, because he could get his fuel into his tanks cheaper than I could. Now if Leazenby was so concerned about enforcing the law on gasoline price fixing, why wouldn't he want to obey the law when hauling fuel? I could only assume that he knew he had nothing to fear about getting caught violating the weight limit laws.

Now when we look at this situation, it becomes apparent that people can make money when deputies are willing to break the law. So how far did it go in the department, and who would be willing to stop any of it if it was brought to proper authorities?

Again, I decided to test the issue. So I contacted Karen Maurer, our county attorney, and presented her with the information I had on the four overloads which Leazenby had pulled in November of 1985. I asked her to check these loads out and prosecute and fine the individual responsible for pulling them on the highway. I also informed her at this point that overloads on the highways were misdemeanor offenses, and required a complaining witness in order to be prosecuted. I then declared myself a complaining witness.

She basically told me she would "look into it" but I heard nothing from Karen Maurer. She had chosen not to prosecute.

I then hired an attorney, Skiles and Butler, and asked them if they would represent me and go up and ask Karen Maurer why nothing had been done about these willful violations of the law. They met with her on July 23rd, six months later, and asked her about it.

She was quite adamant with the attorneys that she was not about to prosecute John Leazenby. Butler told me when he came back to my office that he wondered if there was some connection there. Karen Maurer had almost cried when she said she refused to prosecute Leazenby, and had abruptly ended the conversation and walked out of the office.

Now what needs to be remembered here is that the county attorney has the power to prosecute who they want, and to not prosecute who they want. Whether a crime has been committed or not is no requirement upon their duty to prosecute, they have total discretion. And they exercise this, to whatever benefit they choose.

So I now sought clarification of the law, and how it was enforced, because if Leazenby could do it, why not all the other drivers in the business. If this is the case, I may as well load to the max and save that money too, so I could compete in the same market.

So I wrote a letter to A.G. McClintock, Attorney General, State of Wyoming, and sent copies to the Wyoming Highway Patrol, to Karen Maurer, and to Governor Herschler. I had requested that the State do something to prosecute this and informed them that at the county level, nothing was being done.

I received a letter of response from Lieutenant Cliff Ritchie, Wyoming Highway Patrol. In that letter, Ritchie stated that he felt that the number of violations which the department had written that year was adequate enforcement of that law. I took this to mean that it is not unlawful to pull an overload on the highway unless a highway patrolman needs a ticket to meet the adequate enforcement aspect of the law. In other words, they don't care who pulls overloaded trucks unless they want to care for their own reasons. Therefore, these laws are arbitrarily enforced, and they either want you or they don't, and if they don't want you, the law means nothing. And nobody wanted to charge John Leazenby. Now when the price fixing law came into an enforcement question, any tiny little thing which might have been said or done over a period of five years of the past, or more, could and would be used to prosecute the fullest extent of the law.

Just for curiosity, my driver continued to look into this, looking at carbon copies of load tickets from trash cans at the refineries and bringing the carbons back to our office. By going through them, we were able to determine who was pulling what loads and when, so that we could determine our strategy and decide what we should do to be able to compete. The strategy of asking for law enforcement to keep everybody legal had failed. The amount of money involved here was quite surprising, and for my own records, I decided to keep some of the carbons, but there was really nothing I could do to counter the advantage taken by companies allowing their drivers to pull illegal loads unless I would decide to do it myself, which I chose not to do.

So this is the effect on our society when even our law enforcement deputies break the law, and they know nobody will prosecute them. It puts the monkey on the back of people like me, like a pressure to join them! This is one way that they actually encourage crime. It's a pressure that they put on the public. They get ahead from it, so why shouldn't you?

CHAPTER TWELVE

Regarding my innocence or guilt in the case I've described in this book, one cartoon which I recall from one of the newspapers will always stick in mind. It was a drawing of three monkeys on three gas pumps with the caption, "See no evil, hear no evil, speak no evil." I can't think of a better way for a newspaper to describe the overwhelming belief in town by the public that we were all guilty as rats, all of us gas dealers.

Now, every time I re-read the letter of April 1, 1983, from Richard Dixon, Deputy County Attorney, to Judge Arthur T. Hanscum, it makes me sick. The whole gasoline business is declared guilty. Twice in his letter he refers to schedule A, the Leazenby report. In one reference, "Clearly, my zeal in advocating a grand jury for Albany County is grounded in a appreciation for the investigatory powers possessed by such a body. That these powers are necessary in this case is, I think, adquately demonstrated by Exhibit 'A' and reinforced by the formidable retaliatory measures and means of accomplishing those measures available to the prospective targets of our investigation." Rex Guice is declared a "sacrificial lamb." And "Such a probe would be predicted upon extensive investigative information already developed by the Albany County Sheriff's office which tends to implicate many more parties than the one thus far charged."

Dixon refers to "extensive investigative information" from the sheriff's department, yet the only thing they had was the Leazenby report, which was contradicted by both Dooley and Guice. He called this a competent investigation. It became obvious how fake this report was when we later got to civil trial.

There was no further information as it turned out. The grand jury, quite simply, was formed because Dixon wanted it. Perhaps he felt I was too powerful in town in the gasoline business, and he felt that he wouldn't be able to prove me a criminal because I would use my so-called power to punish

186

anyone who would be asked to testify against me. These assumptions were then linked with a declared public need for cheaper gas. And the two combined resulted in the grand jury.

Now the three monkeys on the pump was an accurate portrayal in the sense that nothing was found in the gasoline industry. However the artistic message was, that we were liars in the business, that we lied to the grand jury, that "we" were some kind of gasoline mafia, a bunch of thugs protecting ourselves with the code of criminals. Is the need for cheap gas so great that innocent people should continue to be held as such in the public eye? Did the newspaper have some duty to clear the air after this? Perhaps to castigate the judge for muzzling the truth in the civil proceeding?

So this letter makes me sick every time I look at it. It was well-crafted, but it was a hoax on the people of Laramie. Can you imagine the instructions given to the grand jurors? They must have been scared to death of me.

But I'll submit this final writing of mine, for the public to read and make judgment. And I will be curious as to who contacts me and what their comments might be. I welcome anyone in Laramie, or anyone anywhere, to speak to me about this and voice an opinion.

Now through the past twelve years, bits and pieces have

187

continued to come to me, usually in some indirect manner, but these bits of opinion have reflected a belief still that I'm every bit the person Richard Dixon created in that letter, and further that there had been a gasoline conspiracy in Laramie, which ironically people somehow believe that Richard Dixon "cleaned up" with his grand jury, even though not a single one of the seventeen indictments regarding price fixing ever carried enough weight to be prosecuted.

Now I must conclude with a recent bit of comment which came to me because I think it appropriately summarizes the effect of this on the community and what the feelings of the community still are, and why it was so important to me to write this book and get this out into the open for all to see.

What had come to pass came from a person whom I thought I knew, and thought she knew me, and in particular I thought she was aware of things I had done in the community.

Further I must say that she was on the board of directors of one of the local charities which I had heavily supported for many years, and she knew this about me and we had this professional relationship as well, and whatever she may do personally, it would not affect my feelings for the charity, but the fact that we had this professional relationship carried quite a bit of weight with me.

On October 25, 1995, at approximately 1:30 PM in the

afternoon, a Wednesday, on the Payless parking lot next to Albertsons in Laramie, my brother Bob and sister-in-law Laura happened to be parked next to this person. And they started having conversation, being friends and neighbors, and Bob had mentioned that he was on his way to Hawaii, where he owned a small piece of property in what we think of as paradise, where he has spent the last four years building a home so he would have a place to stay when he went there. He had also mentioned that he and Laura were driving this Daihatsu, which they were in that day, and that they were going to drive it to California and put it on a ship and send it to Hawaii to be used there, because this Daihatsu gets sixty miles to the gallon of gas, and gas in Hawaii is about two dollars per gallon.

Out of the blue, and probably without any thought to whom she was speaking, she said, "I just filled up with gas on South Third Street and paid ninety-eight-point-nine a gallon. Gasoline has been cheap in Laramie ever since the county attorney prosecuted the gasoline dealers for price fixing."

I asked Bob what he'd said in response, and Bob told me that he just looked at her in disbelief. Suddenly she realized who she had said that to. Then he rolled up the window and drove off.

AFTERWORD

This story, in a very subtle way, raises some of the most crucial social and legal issues which face America today. Of primary concern to this author is the issue of people in power having and taking full latitude with their authority, and having zero accountability for their actions.

Consider the missing cocaine from the evidence locker at the sheriff's department in Albany County. Now it has become public record that the son of the sheriff had used cocaine which had been taken from the evidence locker. Now, if this cocaine could be taken and used by a deputy without being detected except by an unexpected audit by an outside agency, it illustrates how easily a similar amount of the drug could be taken by a deputy and used for other illegal purposes as well, such as to plant evidence and entrap an innocent person for drug possession. How could this be controlled?

Consider the Leazenby and Dooley report, which became the vehicle for the formation of a grand jury. Now a simple "what if," would be what if a deputy and a gasoline dealer had conspired to run another dealer out of business? It would be a possible conclusion that a grand jury investigation with the right amount of press coverage would be enough pressure to force the average American to sell out and leave town. In my case, the Leazenby report would not hold up in court. Ultimately, Leazenby was not held responsible to anwer even in civil court for the harmful effects of the report on my life and reputation.

Consider Deputy County Attorney Richard Dixon, who submitted this report to Judge Hanscum, requesting the grand jury and referencing extensive investigative information, when all he really had was that report.

Consider Judge Arthur T. Hanscum, who called the grand jury with little or no true substance to justify the act. He should not have called a grand jury unless there was evidence that a felony had been committed. Price fixing is only a misdemeanor, and not sufficient cause for a grand jury according to the Attorney General of the State of Wyoming. So, the supposed felony was the alleged kickback payments to me. The report was crucial to the formation of the grand jury. And no effort was made by any of these people to substantiate the report prior to calling the grand jury. Why would this happen this way?

Consider that when the Leazenby kickback report was not used in criminal proceedings, and was later called into testimony in a civil trial, the judge of that trial muzzled Richard Dixon from testifying, and thus sheltered all those who either generated or used the report from any accountability or further prosecution under law. Why did Judge Langdon do this?

Justice was not served in any of these proceedings, and Judge Langdon saw to it that it never would be. The real answers should have been brought to public record, for the sake of the public and the community and our society and for the sake of the individuals and their families who suffered because of this set of actions.

When those people in our legal system carry out "justice" in this manner, we, the people of all of America, have to ask ourselves, is our system so corrupt that we are beyond hope as a civilization? Are we beyond the hope of depending on our deputies, our county attorneys, and our judges? The question is raised, because these people in this story took something upon themselves which defied the legal system they were hired or elected and sworn to serve. And then they defied the system again to protect each other. I beg anyone to read this story and feel otherwise.

It is only the people, only the people, who can do something about this by not turning a blind eye to the system as it stands. As long as the people do not demand accountability by those in power, I simply pose one final issue: "Do not ask for whom the bell tolls, for the bell tolls for thee."

Must we live in fear of our system? Must we be afraid to speak out against corruption? Because I believe that it is this fear which will be the undoing of what's left of the American justice system. We have placed so much power in the hands of those who control the badges and robes, that perhaps we are losing sight of our duties as citizens. This is not to be taken as an indictment of everyone in the legal system, but simply to point out that the opportunity is there for those who would abuse their power and the system. And further, to point out that even in such a clear-cut case as this, the people in the system seem to have adopted the criminal code: don't snitch, don't go after one of your own. Now this makes everyone who participates in this fashion accessories to the crime.

If we have a bottom line in America, it is the morality upon which all our laws are based. This includes God's laws, such as axioms against bearing false witness against thy neighbor, such as telling the truth "so help me God." We ask of our judges a higher standard, even than that of law enforcement or prosecuting attorneys. We ask our judges to be fair and impartial and above all, to serve this magic, precious ideal which we call justice.

This story shows how far against that ideal a judge can go, and in the true sense of the criminal code: to let his fellow colleagues go.

I endured this, as one can readily see upon examination of the story, but my desire to prevail was halted by a single but awsome stroke of Judge Langdon. I had, at the least, prevailed in the sense of my willingness to share this story. As I conclude this episode of my life, I close the book on the story itself, and begin the next phase, which is to forgive those who did this to me and my family. As I already know, my family forgave them quite some time ago. And now it will be my task to do the same. As far as society goes, it is for the people to decide how these kinds of issues will be faced in the future. It is the author's wish that this writing will be of benefit to those interested and concerned about the function and secrecy of grand jury proceedings in American justice.

ABOUT THE AUTHOR

Dick Foster came from a pioneer family. His grandfather and grandmother lived in "The Big Hollow," which is near Lake Hattie, in Albany County just outside of Laramie where this story is set. His father was born at Woods Landing (also near Laramie) and his name was James E. Foster, better known as "Ted." His mother's name was Viola A. John, who came from Pocatello, Idaho. After their marriage, they decided to homestead one hundred and sixty acres of ground at the foot of Jelm Mountain, just across the Laramie River from Woods Landing. He is one of five sons, number three in age, and the only one not born in Wyoming. His two older brothers, Ercell and Bob, were born in Wyoming. But Dick's mother and father had travelled to California and were there when he was born, in a hospital in Los Angeles. Their stay in California had been short because their real roots and desires were in Wyoming, and it was shortly after Dick's birth that they returned to Wyoming and homesteaded the place near Woods Landing. His two younger brothers were then born, Tommy and Clifford. Ercell and Tommy, as of this writing, are deceased.

When Dick became of school age, there had been a log cabin about a mile north of Woods Landing toward Laramie which had been used as the schoolhouse. And the Fosters lived approximately three-quarters of a mile up-river from Woods Landing, which meant a one and three-quarter mile walk each way to school. The only three children in the school were his two brothers and himself, taught by one teacher. He attended this school through the fourth grade, at which time the family moved to Laramie. Like so many stories which circulate about winters and the walk to school in Wyoming, Dick's memories are parallel: he can recall his two older brothers helping him and sometimes having to carry him to get through a bad snow in winter on the way to school.

His mother had fought for years to keep the school open near Woods Landing so her children would have a place to attend, but this struggle had been difficult because the general feeling by the people around Woods Landing was that it would be a waste to try to educate a Foster.

There had been times when the family only had a one-room cabin there at the homestead, and the three brothers (Ercell, Bob, and Dick) had slept in a tent below the cabin. Even in winter. But Dick had the advantage: he got to sleep in the middle. It was later that his father finally constructed another room onto the house and furnished it with a wood stove, which became a bedroom for the boys.

A blessing had been the water. They probably had the best water in the world. There was a spring which came out of the side of Jelm Mountain on the homestead, and water from the spring flowed right by the cabin in a little stream. The Fosters built a small dam with a three-inch hose through which the saved water could flow into a bucket. This was important partly because wells in the area were unthinkable at the time. Nobody could have afforded one. Still today, Bob lives in a nearby draw and he pipes water from a nearby spring directly into his house.

The old outhouse had been fifty yards below the cabin. One of the necessary items had been the old Sears Catalog, for reading and other such purposes as one could find.

Woods Landing today is still a tiny community, mostly inhabited by people from Laramie who prefer to live in the country at the base of the mountains.

After several years at the homestead, Mrs. Foster made the decision that it would be best for their five sons if the family moved to Laramie, where they could all attend school and get a better education. When they first moved to Laramie, they lived on the west side, which was the least expensive place to rent a house.

Dick then attended Lincoln School through the sixth grade. After that, his mother enrolled Ercell, Bob, and Dick at Prep, which is a school on the grounds of the University of Wyoming. This had been possible because he had come from rural Wyoming and the school had been somewhat oriented in that direction with its curriculum. He attended this school through the ninth grade.

He then transferred to Laramie High, where he graduated in 1944. His brother Bob continued at the Prep school and graduated there, and his brother Ercell quit school while in tenth grade. It just so happened that Bob and Dick were the only sons out of five who finished high school.

In 1942 Bob joined the Naval Air Corps, where he completed the pilot training program and got his wings in Pensacola, Florida. He amassed considerable flying experience including landings on aircraft carriers, which he had described as "landing on a postage stamp in the middle of the ocean." Only when Dick later got his pilot's license did he fully understand what Bob had meant.

When Dick finished high school, he faced the draft for WWII, and rather than wait to be drafted, he enlisted in the Navy, and by November of 1944 served in Farragot, Idaho, in Navy Boot Camp. After boot camp, he had been sent to

Washington DC to learn to become a laundryman at sea, which was the trade they had chosen for him because he had worked before in this capacity at the New Method Laundry and also at Quality Cleaners in Laramie. The Navy had wished to capitalize on this previous experience, and thusly, this was Dick's trade in the Navy.

He then was sent to Treasure Island, California to be assigned to a new ship. The entire crew for the USS Norris DD859, had been gathered on the island and then transported by train to Long Beach to put this new ship into commission.

The ship then went from Long Beach to San Diego, then to Pearl Harbor in Honolulu, then on to the South Pacific, to Hong Kong. The ship served as the mail run from Hong Kong to Shanghai for approximately six months after the war had ended. In one incident, he had survived a typhoon in the straights between Japan and the China coast.

His return to the States had come about in a transfer to the USS Bristol, in Hong Kong at the time but making ready for a goodwill trip back to Charleston, South Carolina. The route had been by way of Singapore, then to Ceylon, India. The captain, before getting to Ceylon, had deviated slightly off course to take the ship over the equator, which made all the crew "shellbacks." At the equator, the ship stopped and lowered three lifeboats, enabling Dick and those of the crew who wanted it, to go for a swim. The ship then went to Ceylon, where the poverty of the people of India made quite an impression. Dick had realized that there he had seen real poverty, much more so than Woods Landing or the west side of Laramie, Wyoming. The ship then went to Aden, Arabia, then to the Red Sea, and through the Suez Canal to the Mediterranean Sea. They then set port in Alexandria, Egypt, where they spent three or four days, where the captain had offered a three day pass to Cairo, which Dick accepted. He went through the Great Pyramids, saw the Sphinx, and got bitten by the only camel he ever rode.

The ship then went to Naples, Italy, then to Marseille, France, then through the Straights of Gibralter, then to the Island of Madeira, north of the Canary Islands in the Atlantic, belonging to Portugal. It was on shore patrol in Madeira that Dick had been offered a free glass of fine Portuguese wine at every bar that he patrolled. By the time he had returned to the ship, he had become completely drunk. His supply officer had also been officer of the deck, and they were friends, or Dick may have been in trouble. From there it was across the Atlantic to South Carolina, which completed his trip around the world with the navy, leaving from the Pacific coast, and returning on the Atlantic coast.

Upon discharge in Charleston, Dick had the option to either

take money or a plane ticket from the navy to get back home. He took the money, along with other pay he had coming (which was substantial since he'd drawn very little pay overseas). He had also saved money which he had earned on the side doing special laundry with whites and blues for other sailors when they would put into port. Officers got this free, enlisted men had to hire Dick or do it themselves. So, with this money, Dick bought a new car to drive home. One experience with that car should have told Dick that his problem of drinking had the potential of ruining his life. He and another sailor had gone out on liberty and drank heavily, winding up passed out on the beach in the car. When he awoke, he realized that the tide had come in and the saltwater was already up inside the new car. The car started but couldn't move because of the force of the water and the sand. He ran about a mile to the nearest wrecker, and upon return had to swim out to the car with the tow cable, still dressed in his navy whites. He hooked onto the car and the wrecker pulled it to shore and towed it to the shop.

The next morning the mechanic cleaned the car up pretty well and changed all the fluids. It ran, but within a few weeks the body began to tell the tale of the saltwater effects and showed rust. By the time he got home in the new, 1944 convertible he had already made the decision to trade the car for another one before the rust ate everything but the steering wheel. Of all the money he'd saved and earned in two years in the navy, this one incident had taken over half of it. Like with so many men who got started drinking, this first clue had gone unheeded.

Back in Laramie now, Dick had gone to a dance at Gray's Gables, a dance hall east of town about two miles. He loved to dance and it was there he met a young lady by the name of Dorothy Mae Fosdick, originally from Hanna, Wyoming. In the course of the next three or four months the two became married. After a little over a year, Dorothy gave birth to twin girls, Judy and Trudy. Dick had gone back to work for New Method Laundry again, as he had before the service, and he drove a route from Laramie to Hanna, which also included stops in Bosler, Rock River and Medicine Bow. He usually spent the night at the Hanna Inn and returned the following day. It was on one of these nights away that the twins had been born. Two of his friends had come to Hanna to find Dick and found him at Red's Bar in Elmo, an adjacent town. Dick frequented Red's and played slot machines and drank heavily. He was also a regular at the Tuesday night poker games. Dick had been quite a target for easy money due to his alcohol problem and sometimes lost the entire week's pay.

The two men who came to get him had been Bill Wyatt

(later to become a brother-in-law) and Donald Nickerson (now a neighbor in Mesa, Arizona during winter months). It took the two men over an hour to convince Dick that Dorothy was in labor with twins, as they hadn't been expecting this until the following month. So by the time they got Dick to Laramie, Dorothy was already in the delivery room so he hadn't been able to see her until after the births. And then there was the expense of the pair, which was substantial due to incubation and special medical care requirements of tiny size and premature birth. Dick had no money at the time and had to make payment arrangements with the hospital.

Shortly after the twins were born another incident occured, this time in the housing development where they lived, Veterans Village near Stink Lake, now a city park but then a set of houses built by the government for GI's returning from the war. Dick had come home drunk and gone to bed with cigarette in hand, which fell on the mattress and set it afire. If the twins hadn't awakened with the smoke and cried out, Dorothy may not have awakened as she did and they probably all would have suffocated. The smoldering mattress had filled the entire house with thick smoke and Dick and Dorothy dragged it out into the parking lot in the night. This should have been another clue that his drinking was a problem, this time endangering the lives of his family, but again, the warning went unheeded.

The result was that Dick and Dorothy, married only two years, got divorced. Dick's grandmother, Martha Rourke, had visited his mother in Laramie at the time and Martha offered to help Dick straighten his life out. So Dick went to San Jose, California with her. It wasn't right then that Dick faced the alcohol problem in such a way as to beat it, but Martha had certainly played an important part in the process. She had given part of her life to help Dick see what his life could be, if in fact he wanted to be different. She had said to him, "If you'll straighten your life up, with your ability to work, I could make a millionaire out of you in five years."

It didn't take hold at that point, but the memory of that sentence stayed with him. After eight months in San Jose, Dorothy and Dick decided to try to get back together, mostly for the sake of the twins. Dorothy had asked if he would quit drinking, and he'd said he would, not meaning it to be a lie, but he did make the commitment.

He had missed his wife and his children and had certainly realized just what they meant to him. So Dorothy and the kids came to San Jose and Dick in the meantime had secured a job with Standard Stations Incorporated, a subsidiary of Standard Oil Company. Martha had made part of her house into an apartment, which the Foster family rented from her. Although

Dick had not quit drinking completely, he had controlled it somewhat.

But suddenly, in the last two weeks of his inactive duty in the Navy Reserves which he'd signed onto upon discharge in Charleston, Dick was called back into the navy. He was told he had no say in the matter, that he would have to serve another year, and the orders were to report to Treasure Island again. The Korean Conflict was on.

The letter had come in effect from Harry Truman, giving him ten days to report. Needless to say, married with two children, divorced, and then reunited with his family, he had absolutely no desire to go back into the Navy. But he did his duty and reported to Treasure Island as requested. In just six days he was assigned to duty on Kwajalein, an island (atoll) in the West Pacific in the Ralik chain of the Marshall Islands.

So, just sixteen days from the receipt of the letter in San Jose, Dick was back in the navy and back in the South Pacific. His tour of duty was to be one year, and he spent exactly one year and one day. Since the laundry on the island was tended to by the natives, Dick was assigned to store duty, where he became the manager of the beer supply house. To imagine Dick in this capacity was to imagine a pyromaniac in a match factory. Because of prior thefts and the nature of the beer warehouse,

Dick had been asked to build quarters right there inside the warehouse and live there to enhance security. So this he did, even designing a system to catch rainwater from the roof for his own inside shower.

As it came to pass, shipments of beer would come in on flatbed trucks, consisting of about ten thousand cases loaded one hundred cases per pallet. Dick would unload the shipments with a forklift and the help of one native by the name of Moody with whom he became great friends. The beer was then sold by the navy to the clubs by the pallet, and Dick would load the trucks which came to pick it up. Needless to say, any good drinker involved in any aspect of this process ought to be able to figure out how to get a share of this from pallet to palate. Pick-ups were only allowed on Tuesdays and Thursdays between two and four in the afternoon. So Dick was only required to work four hours a week.

By coincidence, the icehouse was located next door to the beer warehouse, so Dick built a cooler big enough to hold a hundred pounds of ice to keep his food cold, the food of course being beer. He brought his ice in on the forklift, the cooler was so big, and only the imagination could estimate the beer consumption in this ideal setting.

After a year and a day of this, Dick returned to the States via a fourteen-day ship voyage routed through Hawaii and arriving in San Francisco. Standard Oil had been very humane, in that they made up the difference between Dick's navy pay and the salary he would have earned with them during his tour of duty, and sent this money to Dorothy periodically through that year. Dorothy had returned to Laramie to wait for Dick and had managed to save every bit of that money, living off only the navy pay which Dick sent home to her. When Dick arrived in San Francisco, Dorothy greeted him at the dock.

Dick resumed his work at Standard Oil at the same station in San Jose at the corner of Fourth and Santa Clara. He then moved up in the company to manager of a 4A station, one of their largest. This had meant moving several times to different stations in different cities, the last move being to Centerville, now known as Freemont. At that particular point, with the help of his grandmother, the Fosters bought their first home.

During the next two to three years, partly due to the habits formed while drinking excessively on the Marshall Islands, Dick fell into drinking with his friends at night, sometimes until two or three in the morning. Drinking gradually began to come first, and there was no stopping it once Dick got started. The marriage deteriorated accordingly, and it became evident that there would be another breakup if this continued.

The night of June 20, 1956 followed a day off work which Dick had spent at home staining a fence with redwood stain. He had run out of stain and told Dorothy he was going up town to get more. Upon doing so he encountered a friend and employee, John Krouse, who also liked to drink beer, and the two wound up at a bar to have a beer together. As usual, one became two and then three, and after three, Dick lost his self-control, which he did for the rest of that day and into the night. They went to practically all the bars around Centerville and then late that night decided to drive to San Jose, twenty miles to the south, to drink more beer there. No part of this drive can be remembered except the last detail, where Dick drove his car into the back of a semitruck and trailer which had stopped at a railroad crossing. Needless to say, the damage was extensive but luckily neither Dick nor John had been injured. When the police arrived, however, a witness had exclaimed, "My God, they're bleeding to death!"

The can of redwood stain in the car had ruptured on impact and splattered all over them and some could be seen running out of the car onto the ground. The result of the excitement was that Dick was booked for drunk driving and even John was arrested for being drunk with him. They were taken to the San Jose jail where they spent the night and the next morning were allowed their infamous one phone call. Dick had called Dorothy and asked her to come and get him. Her rejoinder stands clear yet today to Dick: "Stay there and rot you son-of-a-bitch! At least I'll know where you are."

Dick had no money for bail so he spent two nights in jail prior to arraignment, where he faced a judge, pleaded guilty, and was sentenced to a three hundred dollar fine or three hundred days in jail (at a dollar per day). The fellow who appeared before him got the same sentence for the same offense, and Dick had heard the judge accept his offer to pay twenty five dollars a month for a year rather than sit in jail, so Dick made the same request and the judge granted him a payment plan and released him that day.

Out of jail, the next immediate concern was the possible effect of all this on his job. He had missed two days without calling in, and in the past he had never missed a day for any reason. When he got home he immediately called and explained and his boss arranged to meet him to discuss it in person and turned out to be very understanding. This sometimes is not the best when it comes to an alcoholic but his boss had mentioned AA and recommended Dick to get in touch with them. Dick acknowledged his alcohol problem and said he'd make contact.

That night he found an ad in the newspaper which read Alcoholics Anonymous and listed a phone number. Now in the fifties, this was almost like a secret society because it was so shameful to be identified with this group. But he made the call and a man by the name of Herb picked him up and drove him to his first meeting in nearby Livermore, twenty miles away.

This was the beginning of the change, and Dick did quit drinking. Part of the key was to have been able to talk with others who had an even bigger problem with this, and for the first time, he realized he wasn't alone with this problem.

Shortly after he quit drinking he quit Standard and started his own Chevron station as a dealer in San Jose. His relationship with Standard was still a good one, but he had now made the transition to become an independent businessman rather than an employee. It was about this time that his son Jeff was born. After running two different stations in this capacity in San Jose, the decision was made to move back to Laramie and go into the service station business there.

From 1959 until the present, Dick Foster has operated gasoline stations in Laramie and in other cities throughout Wyoming, including becoming an oil jobber (which means you can buy fuel directly from any refinery rather than just one oil company). Through this jobber ability, Dick was able to expand into a multi-station operation and into other business enterprises as well, in particular, the motel business.

Dick retired five years ago and still resides in Laramie with his wife Dorothy, and they spend their winters in Mesa, Arizona.